Praise for *Brunch: A History*

"This engaging, informative book traces the history of brunch from its origins as a hunt breakfast for the British elite to the hipster meal par excellence. But the author's scope extends beyond the Anglo-American world to cover brunch in Asia, South Asia, and the Middle East. Her impressive array of sources includes magazines, cookbooks, movies, music, and novels, which make for a delightful account of the meal that has been called one of life's great pleasures." —**Colleen Taylor Sen**, food writer and historian; coauthor/cowriter, *Street Food Around the World: An Encyclopedia of Food* and *Culture and Food Culture in India and Curry: A Global History*

"Why we eat what we eat when we eat are questions that are not always tackled together and rarely is the last one the focal point. In her well-researched and innovative history of brunch, Farha Ternikar leads us through a fascinating culinary journey that ripples out globally over the span of more than a century. When probed through a variety of cultural, social, and temporal prisms, the foods and reasons for selecting them become dislodged from our mundane menus to become symbolic markers of an engrossing, wider narrative." —**George Solt**, assistant professor of history, New York University

"*Brunch* turns out to be a great story, intricate and full of surprises. This book takes us out for a rich meal in a fine restaurant and also into the intimate ritual of the family at home. Like the meal itself, *Brunch* is an eclectic and flexible mix, relating the history of many things today taken for granted." —**Richard Wilk**, Provost's Professor of Anthropology, Indiana University

"After the hour-long wait for the perfect eggs Benedict, read *Brunch*. Ternikar's fascinating book shows us how the world's newest mealtime spread across the globe, from Emily Post at Delmonico's to Dubai. Beyond comfort foods and weekend indulgence lies a powerful history of class, colonialism, family, and home." —**Daniel Bender**, professor and Canada Research Chair in Cultural History, University of Toronto

BRUNCH

The Meals Series
as part of the Rowman & Littlefield
Studies in Food and Gastronomy

General Editor: Ken Albala, Professor of History, University of the Pacific (kalbala@pacific.edu)

Rowman & Littlefield Executive Editor: Suzanne Staszak-Silva (sstaszak-silva@rowman.com)

The Meals series examines our daily meals—breakfast, lunch, dinner, tea—as well as special meals such as the picnic and barbeque, both as historical construct and global phenomena. We take these meals for granted, but the series volumes provide surprising information that will change the way you think about eating. A single meal in each volume is anatomized, its social and cultural meaning brought into sharp focus, and the customs and manners of various peoples are explained in context. Each volume also looks closely at the foods we commonly include and why.

BRUNCH

A History

Farha Ternikar

ROWMAN & LITTLEFIELD
Lanham • Boulder • New York • London

Published by Rowman & Littlefield
A wholly owned subsidiary of The Rowman & Littlefield Publishing Group,
Inc.
4501 Forbes Boulevard, Suite 200, Lanham, Maryland 20706
www.rowman.com

16 Carlisle Street, London W1D 3BT, United Kingdom

British Library Cataloguing in Publication Information Available

Library of Congress Cataloging-in-Publication Data

Ternikar, Farha, 1970–
Brunch : a history / Farha Ternikar.
pages cm—(The meals series)
Includes bibliographical references and index.
ISBN 978-1-4422-2942-6 (cloth : alk. paper)—ISBN 978-1-4422-2943-3 (electronic : alk. paper) 1.
Brunches—History. 2. Food habits—History. I. Title.
GT2850.T43 2014
394.1'25209—dc23
2014003612

∞™ The paper used in this publication meets the minimum requirements of
American National Standard for Information Sciences Permanence of Paper
for Printed Library Materials, ANSI/NISO Z39.48-1992.

Printed in the United States of America

To Dad, who taught me his love of aloo paratha and keema, weetabix, and marmalade and biscuits. I wish you were here to share brunch.

CONTENTS

SERIES FOREWORD

Custom becomes second nature, and this especially true of meals. We expect to eat them at a certain time and place, and we have a set of scripted foods considered appropriate for each. Bacon, eggs, and toast are breakfast; sandwiches are lunch; meat, potatoes, and vegetables are dinner, followed by dessert. Breakfast for dinner is so much fun precisely because it is out of the ordinary and transgressive. But meal patterns were not always this way. In the Middle Ages people ate two meals, the larger in the morning. Today the idea of a heavy meal with meat and wine at 11:00 AM strikes us as strange and decidedly unpleasant. Likewise when abroad, the food that people eat, at what seems to us the wrong time of day, can be shocking. Again, our customs have become so ingrained that we assume they are natural, correct, and biologically sound.

The Meals series will demonstrate exactly the opposite. Not only have meal times changed but the menu as well, both through history and around the globe. Only a simple bowl of soup with a crust of bread for supper? That's where the name comes from. Our dinner, coming from *disner* in Old French, *disjejeunare* in Latin, actually means to break fast and was eaten in the morning. Each meal also has its own unique characteristics that evolve over time. We will see the invention of the picnic and barbecue, the gradual adoption of lunch as a new midday meal, and even certain meals practiced as hallowed institutions in some places but scarcely at all elsewhere, such as tea—the meal, not the drink. Often food items suddenly appear in a meal as quintessential, such as cold breakfast cereal, the invention of men like Kellogg and Post. Or they disappear, like oysters for breakfast. Sometimes an entire meal springs from nowhere under unique social conditions, like brunch.

Of course, the decay of the family meal is a topic that deeply concerns us, as people catch a quick bite at their desk or on the go, or eat with their eyes glued to the television set. If eating is one of the greatest pleasures in life, one has to wonder what it says about us when we wolf down a meal in a few minutes flat or when no one talks at the dinner table. Still, meal-time traditions persist for special occasions. They are the time we remind ourselves of who we are and where we come from, when grandma's special lasagna comes to the table for a Sunday dinner, or a Passover Seder is set exactly the same way it has been for thousands of years. We treasure these food rituals precisely because they keep us rooted in a rapidly changing world.

The Meals series examines the meal as both a historical construct and a global phenomenon. Each volume anatomizes a single meal, bringing its social and cultural meaning into sharp focus and explaining the customs and manners of various people in context. Each volume also looks closely at the foods we commonly include and why. In the end I hope you will never take your meal-time customs for granted again.

Ken Albala
University of the Pacific

ACKNOWLEDGMENTS

This book would not have been possible without the support of my husband, co-bruncher, and often editor, Travis Vande Berg.

Personal and professional encouragement from Asmaa Malik and Megan Elias made the beginnings of *Brunch* possible.

I also appreciate all the careful assistance from both editors, Suzanne Staszak-Silva and Ken Albala, and am especially thankful for such a patient assistant editor, Kathryn Knigge.

I am grateful to the Le Moyne College community, but especially to Wayne Stevens, Inga Barnello, and Kelly Delevan at Le Moyne College library. Access to Cornell University archives and New York University's Feast and Famine series was also invaluable.

I also thank Patrick Williams, Daeya Malboeuf, Harriet Brown, Jamie Young, Lesley Porcelli, and Jed Ashton for endless resources and creative consulting.

Thank you for all the brunches that supported this project, especially those at Alto Cinco in Syracuse, Hattie's in Saratoga, and North Star in Ithaca.

Lastly, thank you to Deeba, Saba, and Ammi for all the brunches we've shared from London to Syracuse to New York City.

INTRODUCTION

Lobster Benedict, fried chicken and waffles, or dim sum all exemplify the decadence and diversity of brunch. Who brunches and what we enjoy for brunch have changed since brunch's recent invention, but brunch remains the weekend meal of comfort and indulgence.

Brunch is a somewhat modern ritual, with its first mention coming from Guy Beringer in an 1895 magazine article, "Brunch: A Plea." The meal originated in England, and it spread throughout the United States by the 1920s from New York City, Chicago, and New Orleans. The history of brunch in the United States is a bit unclear. Some evidence suggests the American brunch was created in New Orleans, while others claim that during the gilded age, we saw brunch first take off in New York when city socialites such as Emily Post brunched at the infamous Delmonico's in Manhattan.

The spread of brunch has been shaped by social class, gender, and religious norms. Brunch began on Sundays and then became a ritual shared on both Saturdays and Sundays. Globalization and colonialism both contributed to brunch's spread across the world, especially into parts of Asia and the Middle East, where brunch is often eaten on Sunday but also on Fridays in Islamic and Middle Eastern cultures.

Chapter 1, "The History of Brunch," traces brunch from England in 1895 to the 1980s in the United States. The chapter emphasizes how both religion and gender played an important role in the development of brunch as a social institution. Brunch may have begun as an after-church tradition for English Catholics or as a late Sunday breakfast for Saturday-night pub crawlers, but today it has become a contemporary symbol of culinary decadence and comfort food.

Chapter 2 examines brunch in the United States and the cultural significance of brunch globally. American brunch dishes such as eggs Benedict, omelets, fried chicken and waffles, as well as brunch drinks such as mimosas and the Bloody Mary are featured here. This chapter also explores brunch in Western Europe, Asia, and the Middle East. By looking at brunch across the world, we see how religion, culture, and immigration shape the diversity of brunch times and menus.

Chapters 3 and 4 divide the ritual of brunch between the family meal at home and the public ritual in restaurants. Brunch at home often conjures up images of Christmas or Easter brunch with the extended family, but it also has a history of secular holidays such as Mother's Day and Father's Day.

Chapter 5 explores the appearance of brunch in the arts and popular media. In a *Portlandia* episode of 2012, "Brunch Village," Peter and Nancy line up behind hundreds of others along several streets waiting to eat at the newest hipster brunch spot, "Fisherman's Porch." This sketch highlights and parodies what lengths American yuppies and hipsters will go to just to partake of the latest cultural trends, including eating at the newest hot brunch place. Brunch in popular culture exemplifies how the meal is shaped by gender, class, and shifting social norms.

I

BRUNCH HISTORY

Brunch is the combination of breakfast and lunch, but what makes brunch distinct from breakfast? Breakfast is the beginning of a workday, and brunch marks the weekend. Brunch can include both breakfast and lunch fare because at brunch there are no rules. Brunch lends itself to informality and leisure, culinary indulgences, and comfort food. Brunch is the guilt-free meal when you can have your cake and eat it too, or fried chicken and waffles or eggs Benedict and French toast!

Variations of brunch existed in many cultures for years before the term *brunch* was created. The Chinese have had dim sum (small dumplings) for centuries. The French have a tradition of *le grand petit déjeuner*. In Mexico, huevos rancheros was named after the rancher's breakfast. Even though the term *brunch* was British in origin, brunch became an American tradition as it gained popularity in both New Orleans and New York City. By the 1920s, brunching in upscale hotels had become a symbol of status, and by the 1950s, brunch began to become more of a symbol of comfort and convenience. In more recent decades, brunch has been reimagined as a meal of both comfort and casual entertaining and as an occasion for indulgent and decadent dining. When else do we have an occasion to eat fried chicken and waffles, or oysters and lobster Benedict? Whatever the occasion, from a casual brunch out to catch up with friends or a holiday brunch to connect with the family, brunch is a reason to relax, slow down, and enjoy sumptuous dishes

THE ORIGINS OF BRUNCH: ENGLAND, NEW ORLEANS, AND NEW YORK CITY

The *Oxford English Dictionary* and *Punch* magazine cite the origins of the word *brunch* from an 1895 article called "Brunch: A Plea" by Guy Beringer in the British magazine *Hunter's Weekly*. A Hunter's breakfast was common among the elite in English society and was a late breakfast, usually including a selection of heavy meats, which men enjoyed after a morning of hunting. Hunter's breakfasts

> came to resemble closely what we think of today as brunch; the word brunch first came into use in the English language at around the same time. British journalist Guy Beringer . . . wrote persuasively that "[b]y eliminating the need to get up early on Sunday, brunch would make life brighter for Saturday-night carousers. It would promote human happiness in other ways as well. Brunch is cheerful, sociable and inciting. It is talk-compelling. It puts you in a good temper, it makes you satisfied with yourself and your fellow beings, it sweeps away the worries and cobwebs of the week."[1]

In England, such meals were an indication of affluence. As British families accumulated more wealth, their breakfasts became more extravagant and by the 1880s included savory puddings, pies, meats, sauces, and roasts. This "conspicuous consumption" by the aristocrats further displayed the stratification of British society.[2]

The first print mention of brunch in the United States was just a year after the term was coined in England in a November 27,

1896, special column in the *New Oxford* "News and Notes for Women" titled "The Newest Thing in Lunches":

> The latest "fad" is to issue invitations for a meal called "brunch." This means a repast at 11 o'clock a.m., which is supposed to be the mid-day time between breakfast and lunch. Fashion may be foolish, but it is quite safe to state that if the free lunch had not been knocked out by the Raines law such an epicurean idea would never have been thought of.[3]

Brunch did not become a luxurious, elegant meal until it arrived in the American South,[4] and its first foothold in the United States was in New Orleans in the late 1890s. Begue's in New Orleans is understood to be the first place to serve brunch in the South, and many consider New Orleans to be the original brunch city.[5] Madame Begue was a German immigrant to New Orleans who catered to French merchants, and her "second breakfast" was influenced by both French and German traditions. Many brunch dishes, including Oysters Rockefeller and grillades and grits, and "even the 'brunch time' meal" itself are credited to Madame Begue.[6] Begue's became a notable establishment in terms of New Orleans cuisine and for the development of brunch as an American institution. At Begue's, the staff would serve up both Cajun and French favorites alongside mixed drinks and coffees. Pain perdu, meaning "lost bread" or French toast, was also popularized by Begue's.[7]

Madame Begue may have been the first to serve the "second breakfast" in New Orleans, but in New Orleans brunch quickly took on a life of its own.[8] Brennan's was also a key player in establishing brunch in New Orleans.[9] Classic Southern brunch fare at Brennan's included eggs Benedict, eggs bourguignon, eggs Sardou, omelets with seafood and sweetbreads,[10] as well as absinthe Suissesse, bananas Foster, and hot French bread.[11] Luxurious riverboats on the Ohio and Mississippi Rivers also helped increase brunch's popularity in New Orleans as elaborate brunches were often served on these boats to the elite passengers.

Notable brunch spots in New Orleans include Brennan's and Café du Monde. "In New Orleans, the tradition caught on in the 1950s with Breakfast at Brennan's, where the meals are still lavish, but alas, there is no jazz. Since then Sunday brunch has become de rigueur at the city's large hotels, its flagship restaurants and, increasingly, at more chef-driven eateries . . . from the family-friendly Dixieland jazz at Arnaud's to the you-can-hear-the-tinkle-of-the-silverware setting of the Grill Room in the Windsor Court Hotel to the steeped-in-history brunch at Antoine's."[12] Antoine's is one of the oldest and most famous restaurants in New Orleans. Eggs Sardou (a dish based on eggs, spinach, and artichoke) is credited to Antoine's.[13]

Arnaud's is a restaurant credited with inventing the 1950s brunch cocktail, punch romaine.[14] White rum, Sauvignon Blanc, lime juice, and simple syrup, garnished with nutmeg, is the basis for this brunch drink. The restaurant was established in 1918 by Arnaud Cazenave.

Though the early origins of brunch in the United States can be traced to New Orleans, it is in New York City where brunch was popularized. The infamous Oscar of the Waldorf Astoria in New York City is credited with serving one of the first versions of eggs Benedict, now a brunch staple. New York City's fine restaurants and hotels began advertising lavish Sunday brunches where Manhattan's socialites and upper crust could mingle and dine, and between the 1920s and 1950s, brunch in New York was a meal for the elite. Who else had the time and money to spend on this decadent meal?

In New York City, Delmonico's seems to have been the first institution to serve the glamorous meal that began the tradition of the elite brunch with its menu of Omelet aux fines herbes, poached eggs with truffles, and beignets.[15] The restaurant established social codes of conduct, dress, and demeanor for its guests, and the hosts could turn away patrons at their discretion. Elite upper-class women were the first to be liberated from strict, gendered social norms that often structured public life, and unaccompanied ladies had the privilege to dine at Delmonico's for Saturday and Sunday lunch or brunch. This elite class of women possessed the cultural capital not only to know where to dine but also how to dine in "proper society." Emily Post was observed dining at Delmonico's for a Saturday brunch of oysters, eggs with truffle, filet mignon, and English muffins with her female friends during this time.[16]

EARLY BRUNCH AND THE HISTORY OF EGGS BENEDICT AND FRENCH TOAST

The histories of eggs Benedict and French toast are intertwined with the history of brunch. Eggs Benedict reflects the decadence of the Gilded Age in New York City while pain perdu reflects the French influence of brunch in New Orleans, but who created these brunch dishes?

There is some debate about whether eggs Benedict originated at the Waldorf Hotel or at Delmonico's.[17] According to a 1942 *New Yorker* article, the origin of eggs Benedict can be traced back to socialite Lemuel Benedict ordering a meal at the Waldorf:

> Lemuel Benedict came into the dining room of the old Waldorf for a late breakfast. He had a hangover (the statute of limitations permits publication of this libel), but his brain was clicking away in high gear. He ordered some buttered toast, crisp bacon, two poached eggs, and a *hooker* of hollandaise sauce, and then and there proceeded to put together the dish that has ever since, borne his name. Oscar of the Waldorf got wind of this unorthodox delicacy, tested it, and put it on his breakfast and luncheon menus with certain modifications' Os-

car's version of Eggs Benedict substituted ham for bacon—
and a toasted English muffin for toasted bread.[18]

Others, including Julia Child, claim that eggs Benedict originated
with Chef Charles Ranhofer at Delmonico's and not at the Waldorf. In 1978, *Bon Appétit* credited Mr. and Mrs. LeGrand Benedict as the creators of eggs Benedict at Delmonico's.[19] By the
1970s, eggs Benedict had been adapted into a fast food. In 1970,
Jack in the Box began serving an eggs Benedict sandwich, and in
1971, the eggs Benedict sandwich was modified by McDonald's
to become the Egg McMuffin.[20]

The origin of French toast in the United States has a somewhat
clearer history and can be traced back to Begue's in New Orleans
as pain perdu. Pain perdu was brought to New Orleans by French
immigrants and became what we know as French toast in the
United States. Here we can see the influence of French cuisine
on Louisiana cuisine. American versions of French toast generally

Eggs Benedict (© *Getty Images*)

Chocolate chip orange brioche French toast (*Photograph by Thomas Barwick. © Thomas M. Barwick Inc.*)

involve a simple preparation of frying bread in an egg batter with some sugar and milk. Variations on this often include maple French toast, bourbon French toast, and French vanilla French toast. French toast is often served with maple syrup but can also be served with jam or sandwiched with cream cheese, brie, or other sweet condiments. French toast also has variations across other cultures. In the United States, we often think of it as a breakfast or brunch dish, but in France and India, there are variations of French toast that are more custard-like and are served for dessert.

PROHIBITION AND THE BRUNCH COCKTAIL

Brunch history is also intertwined with the history of cocktails. The temperance movement, which can be traced to the early Women's Christian Temperance Union, was organized by 1874. This movement was led primarily by white Protestant women who sought to outlaw alcohol consumption because it was seen as a moral threat to family values and corrupting American society.[21] In 1919, ratification of the Eighteenth Amendment prohibited the sale of alcohol and the National Prohibition Act of 1919 (more commonly known as the Volstead Act) was enforced for thirteen years from 1920 until 1933.[22]

Though prohibition affected many, the elite were largely unscathed because of private clubs, home bars, and underground methods of transporting and selling alcohol. The mixing of cocktails became common in private homes, private clubs, and elite establishments: "Throughout the 1920s cocktails grew in popularity. Federal dry laws affected the quality as well as the volume of licit and illicit distilled liquor. Mixing helped disguise the fact that the scotch one was drinking had been aged for hours instead of years. Unlike cocktail manuals written before World War I for professional bartenders, Prohibition-era manuals aimed at the enthusiastic novice within the home."[23]

Brunch, a meal that allowed these indulgences, quietly adopted mixed drinks and cocktails. Those who adhered to Prohibition laws may have opted for coffee or tea instead of a Bloody Mary or mimosa, but the alcohol was there for those who wanted it. Many of the earliest brunch cocktails were some combination of vodka or champagne and fruit juices. Citrus juices had already been popularized as a breakfast tradition, so juice-based cocktails were a natural outcome of the combination of Prohibition and brunching, especially with the popular idea that "the hair of the dog that bit you" was the best cure for a hangover.

Some credit the Bloody Mary, one of earliest hangover cures, to bartender Ferdinand "Pete" Petiot at Harry's Bar in Paris in 1921.[24] The origin of the name is a source of some controversy. Others claim that the Bloody Mary was named after Queen Mary I of England, known as Bloody Mary for burning hundreds of Protestants during her rein in the sixteenth century, while another theory is that it came from a waitress named Mary who worked at the Chicago bar, the Bucket of Blood,[25] and still others believe it was named for Petiot's girlfriend.[26]

The mimosa was invented in 1925 in Paris. It is very similar to the English drink the Buck's Fizz, which is also an orange juice and champagne cocktail, but the mimosa is made with equal parts champagne and orange juice while the Buck's Fizz consists of two parts juice and one part champagne. The Bellini was invented in the 1930s at Harry's Bar and got its name in 1948 after the colors used by the painter Giovanni Bellini. Bellinis are made from peach juice and Prosecco, and served in a chilled glass.[27] The Greyhound is a basic brunch drink of grapefruit juice, vodka, and ice.[28] This becomes a Salty Dog if you rub the rim of the glass with grapefruit and dip in salt. Other popular brunch cocktails include the Ramos Gin Fizz and brandy milk punch.

By the end of Prohibition, the upper class had incorporated daytime drinking into their lives, but the middle class wavered in terms of social norms associated with alcohol consumption. Middle-class women in particular were cautioned about daytime drinking and the effect it might have on their reputations. In a section on brunch, the 1937 cookbook *Corned Beef and Caviar for the Live Aloner* discourages the service of alcohol so early in the day: "As for drinks (alcoholic)—unless you feel that your guests want or need them, we wouldn't serve them so early in the day. In fact we wouldn't anyways."[29]

By the 1970s, drinking during the day had lost much of its stigma, even for women, and daytime drinking accompanied the spread of brunch. The brunch cocktail had become a permanent part of most brunch menus inside the home and in restaurants and hotels:

> Though the term "brunch" was coined back in 1895, it fit the laid-back, hedonistic 1970s lifestyle perfectly. Drinks were an important part of the brunch meal, and though bloody marys and mimosas remained popular, new drinks were also invented such as the Elmer Fudpucker and Harvey Wallbanger. Supposedly, the Wallbanger was named after a surfer named Harvey who, after drinking too many Galliano and vodka concoctions, walked into a wall. Crepes, another popular '70s dish, could be served at brunch or any other meal.[30]

THE SPREAD OF BRUNCH IN THE UNITED STATES: THE 1920s AND 1930s

By the 1920s, brunch begins to appear in women's advice columns and etiquette guides. In the 1920s, brunch was still a meal taken in restaurants and public places by the upper class and elite. Tearooms in particular catered to women and ladies who lunched and eventually brunched. In 1924, Ida C. Bailey Allen addressed brunch in one of her early cookbooks in *Mrs. Allen on Cooking, Menus, Service*. Allen refers to brunch as the company breakfast and French *dejeuner* as well. The French dejeuner was actually a lunch that may have been associated with the early origins of brunch, but the company breakfast or breakfast party was a term used for entertaining in the home. Allen gives two sample menus for brunch, including the winter breakfast, which consists of grapefruit, ham, potatoes, toast, waffles with syrup or jam, and coffee and tea, and the summer breakfast, which includes berries, cream, eggs, popovers or potato flour muffins, and coffee.[31]

In 1925, Scotson-Clark in *Half Hours in the Kitchenette: A Self Help for Small Families* explained the difference between breakfast and brunch. On a daily basis, breakfast should be small, but since Sunday is a day of leisure it is an appropriate time for a larger breakfast or "brunch." Sunday lends itself to bacon and other decadent brunch dishes such as finnan haddie (smoked fish), omelets, kidneys, and breakfast meats.[32] In 1927, Della Thompson Lutes's column, "What the Gracious Host Says," explained that, "Any meal that is served before one o'clock is a breakfast. After that, it is called luncheon. There is a fashion now in some tearooms and coffee shops of calling the meal served from ten o'clock to noon, 'brunch' or 'brekko-lunch'—a combination of breakfast and lunch."[33]

During the 1930s there was a transition in brunching from a meal shared in public at hotels or restaurants by the elite of society to a meal that could also be prepared at home. This was especially true for "business girls" and "bachelors," largely because brunch had developed a reputation among the middle class as a meal of ease, convenience, and leisure that didn't require much display in terms of formal china or a dining room. Thus brunch began to be seen as a meal that reduced housework. By the 1930s, housekeepers tight on time, professional women, and artists of the leisure class were all brunching.

By 1932, we see brunch begin to appear in cookbooks. In the women's magazine the *Delineator*, Ann Batchelder suggests that this meal is served between ten in the morning and noon, and that it will allow for a leisurely Sunday but will also keep children and men from getting irritated from hunger. The exact time for brunch can vary, but it is always late morning or early afternoon, and is described as a leisurely meal.[34] Lutes also addresses brunch in *The Gracious Hostess: A Book of Etiquette* in one of the earliest mentions of the wedding breakfast as a type of brunch or breakfast party.[35] Lutes refers to brunch as a fashionable trend only for the upper class, but it had obviously begun to catch on in the United States by the 1930s.

In 1933, the *Washington Post* emphasized that brunch or breakfast parties could also be a meal for those women who were not confident in the kitchen, because brunch did not require the courage that other meals did in terms of preparation. Brunch is also a way for women to entertain either because they are "housekeepers" with limited time or because they are "businesswomen." As Ruth Chambers writes:

> Businesswomen who usually have to eat the morning meal "on the run" on weekdays may enjoy making breakfast a pleasant, leisurely affair on Sundays and holidays and invite their friends to enjoy it with them. Or it just may be the right time for you to entertain some popular guest whose social calendar is crowded with such affairs as dinners, luncheons or afternoon teas. . . . Call them "brunch." . . . Professional people, writers and the people of the theater who are apt to have more leisure at the beginning of the day than the crowded afternoon and evening hours, favor these gay breakfast parties. They are of course somewhat more substantial than the usual light repasts of every day, and in fact, they are like an early luncheon. Someone has coined the term "brunch" to cover these breakfast lunch parties. [36]

By the mid-1930s, brunch begins to be seen as a way to spend holidays and celebrations such as Easter, Christmas, and Mother's Day. Dorothea Duncan, in a 1935 article in the *Washington Post*, suggests for Christmas day to "plan a late combination of breakfast and lunch and serve dinner closer to dusk!" Here, Duncan echoes the trend of housewives receiving domestic advice to start combining breakfast and lunch on Sunday to save time in the kitchen, and maximize time with the family. [37]

In "How We Abolished Week-End Drudgery at Our Home," an article from the *Portsmouth Times* in 1936, Dorothy Marsh writes about taking up brunch on Sundays to cut down on household chores. She explains how she started to serve brunch to save time on domestic chores:

> Now when the family votes for a round or two of golf, a few
> hours in the garden, a long hike, or a swim on Saturday after-
> noon, I am not too busy with dinner preparations to join
> them. . . . As for Sunday, we all have a say as to when its two
> meals shall be served, and never once do we let these meals
> step out of bounds and dictate to us. We're just as well fed and
> lots happier, I know. And Sunday in our house is now a day
> when each one of us has a chance to rest—yes, even I, the
> cook. . . . And I find it an easy way for a business woman to
> entertain without a lot of fuss—for much of the brunch can be
> prepared on Saturday, my day at home.[38]

We can see that brunch becomes seen as something that frees up time by combining breakfast and lunch. This makes more time for other activities and increases leisure time with the family. Brunch can be an easy meal to prepare, especially ahead of time, even for businesswomen, because much of Sunday's brunch can also be prepared on Saturday.

In 1937, Martin Ellyn discussed the spread of brunch in the *Washington Post*: "A mid-morning meal is taking the place of the early breakfasts in many households on Sundays and holidays. This hearty 'brunch' as it is called, is filling and adequate unless there are young children in the family who need meals on schedule."[39] Brunch at home included orange juice, bacon, doughnut rings, coffee, and milk. Though cocktails had become popular by the 1920s, daytime drinking was still not a common social norm.

The spread of brunch was not without some debate, however. In 1936, Emily Post's syndicated newspaper column disparaged "brunch" in a column titled "Breakfast or Lunch." She writes, "I don't know why a meal before 1 o'clock is called breakfast and why at 1 o'clock it becomes a lunch, except that is the way it has always been. At all events, let me implore you not to call your breakfast, at no matter what hour, a 'brunch.'"[40]

In 1939, the *Washington Post* featured another significant article on brunch, emphasizing brunch as a pre- or post-church meal.

The time for Sunday brunch began to shift a bit by the late 1930s as the Sunday supper moved later. The article also declared that brunch was a perfect way to celebrate Easter, as Easter is a spring meal that should be prepared in the home either for before or after church services. Martin Ellyn expands on the popularity of Easter brunch:

> This week brings us to one of the most pleasant ceremonials of the year—Easter. This is the time to glorify Easter in a leisurely fashion. Spring flowers, beautiful silver, lovely linens and other appropriate accessories make an ideal setting for the meal. Easter breakfast is a tradition in Washington, and it is the custom for Washington hostesses to make this meal an occasion for entertaining either before or after church.[41]

By 1939, the *New York Times* declared, "Sunday is a two meal day," a significant proclamation as it symbolized actual changes in meal patterns for at least the American middle class. While the American elite had been brunching since the early 1900s, brunch had now become known as a time saver and economical meal for the American middle class:

> Sunday is a two-meal day with many heathens who concentrate on taking life easy. They sleep late, have a huge combination breakfast and luncheon, and forget the entire subject of food until they think of late supper. The old days when it was customary to get up early Sundays and have breakfast at the usual time, sit down to a huge dinner at noon, and then sleep it off until supper time no longer provide a universal pattern. Hence, the present-day phenomenon of the breakfast—luncheon or "brunch," as it is affectionately called. The word "brunch" is a hybrid, which sticks in the purist's throat. . . . It starts off properly with a breakfast touch—orange or grapefruit juice. Scrambled eggs come next, and with them the pièce de resistance—kidneys and sausages with Madeira sauce, or creamed finnan haddie or chipped beef in cream. This is the dish that distinguishes brunch from ordinary break-

fast. Plenty of strong fresh coffee goes with it, and one finishes
off with a brioche or croissant with perhaps sweet butter and
jam or marmalade or honey.[42]

Brunch had become popular in private clubs and in the homes of
the upper class before it became a meal in restaurants, which
turned it into a social event. *Young America's Cookbook*, published in 1938, called brunch a meal that lends itself to easy entertaining, as it combines cooking breakfast and lunch into one meal.
And in particular, brunch is encouraged as a family meal: "Young
people don't very often have the opportunity to eat away from
home at breakfast time, so why not introduce 'brunch' to your
crowd, and watch how pleased everybody will be."[43]

COOKBOOKS AND HOME COOKING: THE RISE OF THE MIDDLE-CLASS BRUNCH IN THE 1940s

By the 1940s, brunch had become a meal that was both served in
American homes on Sundays and eaten out on holidays and special occasions such as Mother's Day, Easter, and Christmas. With
the popularity of brunch increasing, we started to see an increase
in the number of brunch recipes in cookbooks, since options for
blending breakfast and lunch now were in demand and brunches
came to be seen as a simple, affordable, and convenient way to
entertain at home on the weekend. In addition, advice columns
and etiquette books began embracing brunch because it combined two meals and created more time for leisure. Church attendance was still emphasized as part of the brunch ritual, and Sunday morning "after church" was seen as the ideal time to serve
brunch, according to Bell's *In Successful Parties*.[44] We also continue to see mention of brunch spreading across the nation as a
meal of leisure.

In 1941, in the *Boston Globe*, brunch is described as a leisurely weekly meal where we can "do something tricky with the eggs. The usual orange juice may be missing as such but be supplanted by enticing looking orange water lilies and the bread supply may turn out to be waffles instead of toast, luscious fresh, steaming hot coffee cake, or even English muffins with plenty of butter and marmalade."[45]

Cookbooks dedicated to brunch begin to appear in the 1940s. They emphasized making dishes ahead of time, easy preparation, and combining lunch and breakfast. *The Breakfast and Brunch Cook Book*, published in 1942 by the Culinary Institute of America, is one of the first brunch cookbooks. The cookbook offers recipes, suggestions, and ideas for seasonal, regional, and holiday brunches. "Seasonal Brunches" explains that "brunches follow the breakfast pattern of fruit or fruit juices, eggs, cheese, fish or meat, potatoes, breads, quick breads, and beverages, but use them in luncheon form. . . . Brunch offers really substantial fare, when you have a thick slice of ham broiled crisp at the edges."[46]

"Sectional Brunches" (regional brunches) included selections from Southern brunches such as fruited sausages with hominy, fried apples, American fried potatoes, and mint grapefruit. Midwest brunches included items such as applesauce torte, creamed dried beef, toast timbales, and cinnamon rolls, while Western brunches consisted of baked trout and a fruit plate. New Year's Day, St. Valentine's Day, Washington's Birthday, St. Patrick's Day, May Day, May Garden, Memorial Day, Fourth of July, Labor Day, and Armistice Day are all brunch-appropriate holidays according to *The Breakfast and Brunch Cook Book*.[47] Many of these holiday brunches that began in the 1940s are still popular today. Brunch cocktails were not included in this 1942 cookbook.

Good Housekeeping embraced brunch by the mid-1940s because of the meal's flexibility, diversity, and creativity. In 1945, Katherine Fisher of *Good Housekeeping* wrote:

Sunday should be a day when you and your family can take it easy and make your meal schedule fit your mood. This is why brunch—part breakfast, part lunch—is a good Sunday meal. It can be hearty or light, and it can be served any time. It need not interfere with church or Sunday plans, or with your children's three meals. It can be a sit-down meal or an informal buffet, to which you can welcome the casual guest. Plan an informal evening meal, too. It all helps to make Sunday a day of rest.[48]

Historically, breakfast was a meal that was shared with family or intimate friends, and dinner parties were more formal affairs. Brunch, however, was a new meal that allowed for informal entertaining with guests, and brunch parties or brunch buffets at home lent themselves to relaxed entertaining with acquaintances, work colleagues, or neighbors.

Soon after *Good Housekeeping*'s piece on brunch, *Fannie Engles' Cookbook* was published in 1946. This cookbook explains that brunch is "a combination of breakfast and lunch, served in the late morning or at noon, usually on Sundays or holidays. It is informal, therefore easy to serve. Serve buffet style or set places around the table on the porch or lawn, or before the open fire in cold weather."[49] Under "Appropriate Food," Engles explains that brunch should start with fruit then be followed by a main dish, "hot breads," and coffee. The brunch menus include boiled grapefruit, creamed chipped beef on toast, coffee crumb cake, and coffee, and a second menu included orange juice, French toast, grilled sausages, fruit biscuit rolls, and coffee. Engles made no mention of brunch cocktails in 1946.

SHIFTING GENDER ROLES AND THE SUNDAY AMERICAN TRADITION: BRUNCH IN THE 1950s AND 1960s

By the 1950s, brunch had become a permanent fixture on the menus of most elite restaurants in New York. In 1941, we see brunch on the menu of the Fifth Avenue Hotel as the first advertised brunch menu. By 1950, Tavern on the Green had a Sunday brunch menu that was served from noon to 3 PM. Brunch had become a time-saving meal that was part of the Sunday tradition in America. Theresa Nefy's "We Switched to Sunday Brunch" appeared in 1957 in *Parents' Magazine & Family Home Guide*:

> My husband and I were raised in the tradition of the Big Sunday Dinner. The table groaned with large roasts of beef, two or three kinds of vegetables, potatoes, rolls, preserves, cakes and pies. . . . Finally I decided there must be a better way to plan Sunday meals and activities. We wanted our family together on Sunday, to build the unity so necessary to happy family life. I wanted to skip the long preparation of vegetables. . . . The answer was a Sunday brunch. This is served at noon, when church is over but the afternoon hasn't actually started. The menu is simple, as an early meal should be, and makes good use of convenient frozen foods, mixes and bakery products. We always have fruit juice with mint or fruit or an ice added, then a hot dish followed by Danish or coffee cake, milk for the children, and lots of coffee for adults. The main dish may be a platter of bacon and eggs, or French toast with a choice of jam, jelly, marmalade or honey butter. Sometimes it's hotcakes (we start a little early and have two griddles). Or it may be a huge pile of sausages in biscuit jackets. . . . Yes, at our house the big Sunday dinner has given way to a hospitable brunch—and we love it![50]

Similarly, in Time-Life's *Picture Cook Book* (1958), the author writes:

Today in many families, the big Sunday dinner has given way
to brunch, a leisurely late morning meal that combines the
best of both breakfast and lunch.

Weekday breakfasts are often eaten on the run, but many
cooks find that, on Sunday, brunch followed by a light supper
is more convenient than cooking three meals. It makes the
afternoon much longer and becomes a pleasant time for the
family to get together. Brunch parties are now an accepted
way of entertaining. The menu is usually simpler than for a
luncheon or dinner, and is easier on the hostess since most of
the food can be cooked on short order or prepared ahead of
time. Brunch is a flexible meal that adapts itself to almost any
household. It can be quite formal, a buffet or guests can sit on
cushions around the coffee table. It can be served indoors or
out, with or without alcoholic drinks. . . . But there are no
serious rules for brunch, and some people like to make it more
lunch than breakfast with dishes like chicken casserole, veal or
fish in sauce. It may be accompanied by a simple or even a
fancy dessert, but this is optional; coffee is a must.[51]

Brunch had become a meal with no rules by the late 1950s.
The brunch family meals emphasize diversity of menu choices
and simplification of schedules. Cookbooks suggest brunch's popularity grew because it is one meal replacing two meals, but also it
lent itself to a leisurely Sunday afternoon for more time to spend
with friends or family. Brunch parties appear in the chapter "Bo-
nus Meals from the Piggy Bank" in Ida Bailey Allen's *Solving the
High Cost of Eating: A Cookbook to Live By* (1952). In 1955, the
recipe for "brunch treat" shows up in the *Good Housekeeping
Cookbook* as a smoked turkey sandwich with eggs, biscuits, and
coffee. The authors also mention Sunday brunch: "If you've never
considered this kind of entertaining, do. Sunday brunch is a happy solution for the bachelor, bachelor-girl, or business couple."[52]
And the diversity of brunch dishes continues to increase in the
1950s, going beyond griddlecakes, egg-based dishes, and traditional dinner entrees. In 1955, *Good Housekeeping* magazine pro-

vided recipes for creamed shrimp on rice, deviled ham rolls, mushroom stroganoff, and pumpernickel bread, portraying brunch as a weekend highlight: "May mornings are so delightful that everyone is eager to get up, especially if a Saturday or Sunday brunch for the family or a few friends is in the offing."[53]

Also in the 1950s, as middle-class women aspired to both maintain a domestic life and enter the workforce, brunch was seen as a way to maintain domesticity, and mainstream ladies' magazines and cookbooks continued to take note of brunch as culinary trend. Carl Degler's research highlights why gender roles continued to be important in how and why meal patterns changed.[54] Women's roles in particular contributed to the popularity of brunch among middle-class families. Women entering the workforce after World War II was not the single most important factor leading to the popularity of brunch, but it did contribute to the need for women to find a time and place for leisure. This was the beginning of professional married women who lunched or brunched out. Today ladies who brunch may conjure up images of *Sex and the City* and *Gossip Girl*, but by the 1960s ladies who brunched were often the ladies who worked Monday through Friday. Sunday was the one time that they could find to get out of the house.

By the 1960s, brunch had fully entered the American home, and cookbooks began to appear in larger numbers. Brunch had become a particularly popular way to entertain at home, since it could often minimize preparation and require less resources— egg and bread dishes do not cost as much as meats that were required for formal dinners. In addition, brunch does not require multiple courses unless it is for a special occasion. Of course, special occasions were part of the brunch tradition. Indeed, by the 1960s, the messages about brunch are often conflicting. On the one hand, it can be a simple and casual meal, but on the other hand, it can be a meal of decadence and celebration. Changing gender roles, church attendance, and the legacies of the luxury meals from the 1920s and the thriftiness of the 1930s all contributed to the diversity of brunch in the 1960s.

In 1964, in *American Home*, the authors encourage women to "be a carefree weekend hostess at a brunch":

> Brunch—that ingenious invention of the 20th century—is a rationalized substitute for breakfast and lunch. It fits in perfectly with summer's relaxed way of living. Of course, it takes a bit of creative doing by you to make a seemingly effortless occasion like this come off without a hitch. So plan ahead. Cook in the cool, cool morning, do some things ahead, or choose some of the whip-up-in-jiffy recipes you see here. Use your imagination, unleash your color sense and flair for the unusual. But above all, make the meal a simple offering of delicious, tempting food that will delight their eye and tantalize the taste of late risers and lazy stragglers. Try our tender chicken Amandine, rich with mushrooms and a sprinkling of toasted almonds. For a new twist, serve hot Crab Imperial, a luscious mixture in baked avocado. For those who can't start the day without eggs—ham and eggs au Gratin naturally![55]

By the 1960s, brunch dishes include both breakfast and lunch fare. Egg dishes and coffee drinks make brunch distinct from lunch, but chicken, seafood, and beef all continued to appear in cookbooks, etiquette guides, and ladies newspaper advice columns. In 1966 in *Ladies Home Journal*, brunch is referred to as an American tradition: "Combining breakfast and lunch and then inviting friends over to enjoy it with you—it's an American way of entertaining that's fast becoming an American tradition. Brunch, of course, varies widely in menu and style from one part of the country to another (big-city brunch is apt to be quite formal and elegant, for example). But, in most warm-weather climates, the inclination is toward an outdoor brunch that's wonderfully relaxed and informal."[56]

In *American Home*, brunch is presented as a relaxed way to entertain that avoided evening fuss:

> Nothing's more fun than a brunch—that delicious hybrid served on weekends and holidays in the neighborhood of noon. Not breakfast, not lunch, but a delightful midday get-together where everybody seems to slip into a relaxed, easy-going mood for happy talk, lighthearted food and drink. Californians are longtime practitioners of the fine art of brunching and they are quick with tips and menus that are borrowable straight across the board. The assets of a brunch: no fuss or bother for the host or hostess; no late night stayer-uppers (it's strictly middle of the day); and plain old-shoe comfort for everybody concerned.[57]

But by the late 1960s and early 1970s, there was definitely a shift in gender roles, social norms, and cultural attitudes. In 1969, Helen Gurley Brown's *Single Girl's Cookbook* (after publishing *Sex and the Single Girl*) was one of the first cookbooks aimed at professional single women, but it also addressed somewhat taboo topics such as an overnight guest, entertaining bachelors, daytime drinking, and of course brunch.

> Brunch is a wonderful way for a single girl to entertain. . . . Somehow you don't have to be as good a cook at breakfast (although, by now you are fantastic of course!). Guests are easier to attract for brunch. People will drop by for Sunday breakfast whom you'd feel funny asking to dinner—the popular married couple who are always booked; the couple with children who can babysit with each other in the daytime, no sitters needed; a bachelor in your building who's never even asked to borrow a cup of bourbon but who you feel would like you if he knew you. . . . The timing for brunch is good for a career girl. If you have it on Sunday, you can market, fuss, run up your costume, and do part of the cooking on Saturday. By Sunday noon—most brunches start at noon or one o'clock— you're beautiful, prepared and in command.[58]

Brown's cookbook marked a shift in both entertaining and day-time drinking, and in American culture as a whole. She suggested breakfast recipes for the "almost overnight guest," and gives single girls permission to partake in daytime drinking. "Piffle to the guests who only drink puritanical highballs even at brunch. This morning he'll just have to be more adventurous."[59]

AN "AMERICAN CULTURAL EXPERIENCE": BRUNCH IN THE 1970s AND BEYOND

By the 1970s, brunch had become a permanent American meal and the "anything goes" nature of brunch really embodied the decade's culture. Egg bakes, fondues, and potlucks all lend themselves to casual, no-fuss entertaining. Brunch also allowed for various and diverse styles of menus, cooking, and dining largely because of changes in social norms and relaxed meal etiquette. By the 1970s, brunch had become an American cultural phenomenon.

In 1971's *Let's Have a Brunch*, June Roth writes: "Dear Reader, 'Let's have a brunch!' is often the ideal solution to problems of entertaining whether celebrating a particular occasion or just feeling convivial. . . . Brunch can be as elegant or as easy as you care to make it."[60] In 1972's *McCall's Beautiful Brunch Book*, McClow explains:

> The speed and efficiency of modern, technological life has given rise to an unprecedented amount of leisure time. Brunch seems to be a natural result of the combination of informality and free time. Paradoxically, though the weekends are becoming longer and freer from household chores, the work-week has become more and more demanding. After a hectic week, rising late and enjoying a relaxed, midmorning brunch is a refreshing way to begin a weekend.[61]

The late 1970s continued to embrace brunch because of its effortless appeal. In 1978, in *The Great Sandwich Book,* Borghese writes:

> Brunch is becoming an increasingly popular meal, and perhaps the most enjoyable of any, because it's served at a relaxed time, usually on Sunday, when blessed leisure hours stretch before you. No food is so tailor-made for brunch time as the sandwich, and the recipes in this chapter run the gamut from the favorite classic French-fried Monte Cristo Sandwich, stuffed with ham, cheese and chicken, to new and lively sandwiches like Tipsy Sardines with Mushrooms on Toast. . . . Serve your brunch-time sandwiches with piping-hot coffee, good tea, or steaming chocolate. Start off with juices or, for a more spirited repast, Bloody Marys, Screwdrivers, Salty Dogs (grapefruit juice with vodka and a dash of salt), or any other cocktail that seems appealing for the first meal of the day. If you want to go all out, serve champagne or a chilled white wine with your brunch.[62]

By the end of the 1970s, brunch is popular at restaurants, brunch cookbooks have taken off, and brunch continues to be served at home and hotels. Sunday brunches remain an occasion, but more casual weekend brunches also begin to pop up all over the country even in smaller towns and in the Midwest.

Krasnow expands on the importance of brunch as "America's brave new meal" in 1980 in the *Chicago Tribune:*

> You do not eat brunch. You do brunch. It is the first taste of Sunday, sweet Sunday, after Saturday night. It is an event, a champagne celebration. A meal so important, it has replaced an American classic, the Sunday dinner.
> . . . Where did we get this brave new meal? The brunch borrows from the English hunt breakfast, a lavish board of eggs, meat, chicken livers, bacon, kidneys, fruit with cream, and sweets. It has some of the elements of smorgasbord, with its meatball, pickled herring, and rice pudding. Or the Italian

pranzo: a little bitta pasta, a little bitta wine. With a smattering of a Greek style family dinner: spinach cheese pie, fish roe, yogurt with honey, and the Bavarian breakfast: potato sausage, salad and black bread. Oh yes, of course, it has a French tone: croissants, jam, and café au lait. . . . America, we have invented a new meal. With the loosening of Sunday's rigid schedule of church and dinner, a relaxed and informal brunch is a reflection of this freedom. But brunch, like all good things, was a long time coming. . . . And maybe because anything goes, people adore it.[63]

By the 1990s, brunch became so popular in many cities that hotels and restaurants began offering Saturday brunches as well. Sunday remains the traditional day for hosting brunch in the home, but the idea of a brunch including savory proteins, sweet pastries, and the option for daytime drinking all had such great appeal for Americans that Sunday brunch really became "weekend brunch" at many establishments. Even today at popular brunch spots in New York City, such as Sarabeth's, Cookshop, and Bubby's, serve both Saturday and Sunday brunches.

Though brunch history is very much embedded in traditions of the English and French, in the next chapter we see how brunch remains an American tradition but also goes global by the 1990s. But we can also argue that brunch has existed for centuries outside the United States in China as dim sum and in Mexico as the rancher's second breakfast. If we trace brunch traditions around the world, we get a sense of how popular and global this meal actually is. The Western notion of brunch really began in England, quickly spread to the United States, and finds variations in France, India, Korea, and even in Dubai where Sunday brunch is now a cultural event! Contemporary global variations of brunch can be as diverse as dosas, curried eggs and gulab jaman to shrimp dumplings, chicken feet and sticky rice.

2

CULTURAL IMPORTANCE IN THE UNITED STATES AND AROUND THE WORLD

Brunch began in England in the 1890s but quickly spread to the United States and then to other parts of the world, especially to cultures that have been influenced by colonialism, immigration, globalization, and transnationalism. While in the United States we may be brunching on eggs Benedict and mimosas or fried chicken, waffles, and a latte, there are many diverse interpretations of brunch food around the world. In China, and on the East and West Coasts of the United States, we have the Chinese brunch tradition of dim sum, which includes small plates of sweet and savory steamed or fried dishes. In India, Sunday brunch often includes aloo puree (curried potatoes and fried chapattis); eggs cooked with onions, spices, and pepper; and lassi (yogurt drink). In Dubai and in other parts of the Middle East, brunch is a Friday midday post-prayer meal. By looking at brunch across the world, we also see how religion and culture shape the diversity of brunch times and menus. One thing for certain is that brunch continues to signify comfort or decadence no matter where in the world it is being eaten.

In the United States, both New York City and New Orleans had established strong brunch traditions by the 1920s:

Who cooked the first verifiable American brunch, and where, is a matter of speculation. A New York cook, or one in New Orleans? Whichever was first, the tilt is toward the South. In the mid-1800s, Creole market workers in New Orleans began a late-morning custom of eating a gargantuan second breakfast at Begue's, a coffeehouse. Later, wealthy residents began frequenting Begue's for their late, and leisurely, Sunday breakfasts. What is probable is that by the mid-1930s brunch had become an American custom, despite Emily Post's disapproval. She wrote in an early edition of her books on American etiquette, "But do not give encouragement to that single-headed, double-bodied deformity of the language, brunch. . . . Brunch, breakfast at lunchtime, calls to mind standees at a lunch counter, but not the beauty of hospitable living."

On the contrary, today's brunch is the epitome of gracious entertaining. With a leisurely approach and the inclusion of easy-to-prepare foods, brunch becomes the host's response to the hurried pace of modern American life, a time when he or she can shine.

Its flexible format allows varying degrees of informality: besides offering delicious, well-prepared foods, the cook can be creative with imaginative table settings, dramatic center-pieces, and decorative garnishes. Brunch can also be a communal effort, a time when guests can help cook and serve.[1]

THE CULTURAL IMPORTANCE OF BRUNCH IN THE UNITED STATES

Weekend brunch is as American as Sunday football. Historically, Sunday was a day of rest and relaxation in the United States, especially among the middle and upper classes. After World War II, there was a decline in church attendance, which some suggest contributed to brunch's popularity. By the 1950s in the United States, brunch had become a Sunday ritual after church or as an alternative to church, especially among middle-class families. Brunch became a time for families to have a meal together, often in place of having three meals a day or as a substitute for a sit-down Sunday supper. Women were increasing in numbers in the workforce outside the home, so brunch often lent itself to a more relaxed and minimized preparation for working mothers and wives. Brunch was also a chance to experiment in the kitchen. But most important, brunch became a meal of leisure, comfort, and often decadence in the American cultural imagination.

In American culture, there are many reasons to brunch—from celebrations to weekly family meals. Occasions for brunching include New Year's Eve and even the Fourth of July. Holiday brunches such as Easter and Christmas brunches can be traced back to the early 1900s, and by the 1920s, bridal brunches had become part of wedding traditions. The practice of brunch in the United States is also connected to the social custom of celebration. Civitello explains that "brunch, a traditional way to celebrate Mother's Day, is purely an American invention. The word—brunch—a combination of breakfast and lunch—was not even in the Oxford English Dictionary until recently, although it was in American dictionaries. It originated during the Gilded Age in nineteenth-century America, when women began to have 'breakfast parties.'"[2] The Gilded Age was a time when the elite displayed their wealth via conspicuous consumption, which included hosting breakfast parties and extravagant brunches. It was only the very wealthy who could really afford the time and multifood courses for brunch during its early inception.

In 1914, Mother's Day became an official American holiday,[3] and in 1948, the *Philadelphia Tribune* described an ideal Mother's Day brunch:

> What could be more fun than . . . morning brunch for the whole family on Mother's Day? Brunch is a sort of glamorous, leisurely, combination of breakfast and lunch that is more hearty than an ordinary breakfast. In fact, it often includes a dessert too. Start the menu with grapefruit shells filed with icy

cold grapefruit sections and with fresh or frozen strawberries. A fluffy omelet with a tomato and ripe olive filling is quite delicious with crisp bacon curls and broiled canned cling peaches.[4]

Then, in 1966, President Lyndon B. Johnson established the third Sunday in June as Father's Day and a national holiday,[5] and by the 1960s, both Mother's Day and Father's Day were occasions for brunching.

In 1948, Lynn Stewart wrote about brunch in *American Home* magazine as a New Year's tradition and a family meal that could be used to convene a family meeting: "It is always served at 1 pm. The first course is always citrus juice (orange or grapefruit), and the main course is 'griddle cakes' served with fruits, butter, honey syrup, cottage cheese and nuts. This is accompanied with cinnamon toast. After brunch there is an 'annual family meeting' in which everyone shares annual new year's resolutions."[6]

Brunch omelet (© *cocoaloco*)

Brunch serving as a vehicle for family meetings was not a new idea, as meals were always a way to bring families together. But New Year's brunches began as family brunches and evolved into festive brunches often including friends as well.

When many of us think of holiday brunches, Easter brunches are the first ones to come to mind. By the 1950s, the tradition of the Easter brunch often included an Easter egg hunt as well as a reason to gather the extended family for a sit-down meal. In a 1958 *New York Times Magazine* article, Claiborne described Easter brunch as a leisurely family meal:

> Although the word "brunch" may still strike certain ears as a profanation of the English language, the meal which bears the name can be counted among the pleasanter aspects of Sunday and holiday eating. Because of the hour at which brunch is served—generally between 11 am and 1 pm it can be the most unhurried of meals. . . . The four Easter menus include bloody Mary, eggs Benedict and coffee, bulldozer with melon balls and kedgeree (cooked codfish with rice and eggs), whiskey sour with kippered herring, eggs toast and tea, and cham-pagne, smothered shad roe (the northern fish and egg sack), bacon, toast and coffee.[7]

By the end of the 1950s, almost any occasion became a reason to brunch. In *Parent's Magazine's*, "The Family Home Guide" in 1959, we are given some interesting suggestions for a Fourth of July brunch party:

> One of our favorite get-togethers is the breakfast or brunch party. The children are fresh and rested for the occasion. Also, it's easy to turn breakfast into a special treat at very little cost. . . . What shall we have to eat? The choice is endless, but tiny pancakes, stacked high, are sure to please. I usually use a buttermilk pancake mix for these and put the batter in a pitch-er for easy pouring, onto the hot griddle, set on our back yard grill. Crisp, brown pork sausages are brought from the kitchen

at the strategic moment along with a pitcher of milk for the children and lots of steaming fresh coffee for adults.[8]

This includes recipes for sour cream waffles and party popovers.

By the 1960s, brunch in the United States became a time to catch up with friends and family, or a meal to mark a special occasion. In 1968, Lillian Langseth-Christensen and Carol Sturm Smith explained: "Brunch is usually eaten in the middle or late morning, and because the middle or late morning is usually spent at a desk or on a job, brunch becomes a holiday or a weekend meal and should be something special, shared with friends or as a problem-solver for the weekend-hostess—or as a special treat for the family."[9] Brunch in the United States can consist of steak, potatoes, and eggs, or bacon and pancakes, or eggs Benedict and French toast with a cocktail or a large cup of coffee. Brunch is often an excuse to gather the whole family for a meal. By the 1960s, the brunch supper had lost its significance, and Sunday brunch took on a larger role in bringing the family together for a meal.

In addition to national holidays, weddings also became a reason to brunch. According to *Emily Post's Wedding Etiquette*, the wedding brunch became a cultural tradition for many American families and was often part of a bridal weekend, especially for out-of-town guests.[10] The bridal brunch was usually hosted by the bride's family in the town in which the wedding was thrown. However, in more recent years bridal brunches have gone out of fashion with the increase of destination weddings and the trend away from hosting weddings in the bride's hometown.

By the 1980s, Sunday brunch had become weekend brunch, and a way to mark almost any occasion in American culture: "Now, around noon on almost any Saturday or Sunday, people in America can be found having brunch at home, in restaurants, and in hotel dining rooms. . . . Brunch is also a fashionable way to celebrate occasions such as Easter Sunday. They are also often

Eggs Florentine (*Photo by Heather Bohn-Tallman; http://hbtphoto.pass. us/hatties-brunch-1/i-FBFfT77949769 from Heather Bohm-Tallman photography***)**

given the day after a big event, such as a wedding or a big home-coming sports event, especially if a number of out-of-town guests have not yet left for home."[11] Brunch on Saturday or Sunday could signal a special occasion, a religious holiday, or simply a long weekend.

CLASSIC BRUNCH FARE IN NORTH AMERICA

In the United States, classic brunch fare varies by region, culture, and even decade. Classic brunch fare includes egg dishes as simple as small-town Midwestern egg bakes or as decadent as lobster Benedict, usually accompanied by breakfast meats such as sausage, corned beef hash, or bacon and caffeinated or fruit drinks such as coffees, teas, juices, and cocktails.[12] The diversity of American brunch dishes can be seen through regional traditions. We can trace brunch dishes including the omelet and pain perdu to the New Orleans institutions of Begue's and Brennan's. In Maryland, crab Benedict can't be missed, while in Maine the lobster Benedict is served all year round. In the Southwest, we often sample multiple variations of huevos rancheros, migas, and breakfast burritos for brunch. In parts of the United States, we often include roast beef, smoked fish, and even fried chicken at brunch.

Bagels can be traced to the lower east side of Manhattan in the last nineteenth century and first became popular in the Northeast. Breakstone's cream cheese helped popularize the cream cheese *schmear* and bagels became an early New York City brunch food by the 1920s.[13]

The donut craze took off in 2012 and helped repopularize fast-food donuts from places like Dunkin Donuts and Krispy Kreme but also contributed to the rediscovery of donuts as artisan pastries. Some claimed that donuts were the new cupcake,[14] while others claimed that this was just another food cycle. Gourmet

Breakfast burrito (*Photo by James Young; www.jamieyoungphoto.com/ contact%201.html*)

donuts can be found at Doughnut Plant, Dumont, Buttermilk, or Dough in New York City,[15] and at places like Jim Lahey's Sullivan Street Bakery you can have a bomboloni, a small artisan donut filled with crème or jam, with your weekend brunch.

In Washington, D.C., by 2012, the donut trend materialized into two donut and chicken spots,[16] while in Florida, you can enjoy artisan donuts at Dough or Piquante in Tampa. More recently, Dominique Ansel's hybrid donut and croissant, the "cronut," caused a culinary panic with donut aficionados lining up outside his pastry shop for a sampling of the famed pastry.[17] Cider donuts are all the rage in the fall in Upstate New York. These cake-like donuts are made with apple cider and are usually sprinkled with cinnamon. In Syracuse, we also find seasonal baked donuts using local ingredients at Picasso's Pastries, where you can

Donuts in Upstate New York (*Photo by Kayla Brandt*)

sample pumpkin or sweet potato donuts, in addition to chocolate cake ones.

Scrapple (also a regional brunch food), sometimes known as Panhaas in parts of Pennsylvania, has its roots among the Pennsylvania Dutch. Scrapple has many variations, but is traditionally prepared as a loaf of pork and cornmeal and then fried.[18] It might be best described as the "meatloaf of the morning."[19] Scrapple was historically eaten as a breakfast dish but today is eaten as breakfast or brunch in parts of Pennsylvania, Ohio, and the Mid-

Picasso's chocolate donuts (*Photo by Kayla Brandt*)

west. Today in Philadelphia you can find polenta scrapple, scrapple with poached eggs, and even scrapple sliders.[20]

Common Southern brunch dishes range from grits and eggs to biscuits and sausage with gravy to fried chicken and waffles. Fried chicken and waffles are often thought of as a Southern dish but can also be found in New York City and Washington, D.C. The earliest meat and waffle combination appears in Pennsylvania Dutch country during the 1600s, when the Dutch cooked waffles and topped them with pulled pork or chicken. Fried chicken is often traced back to the seventeenth century in Virginia, when there is evidence of it being served on plantations.[21] "A different, decidedly soul food–inspired approach to the pairing worked its way into popular culture much later with the opening of Wells Supper Club, known simply as 'Wells' to regulars, in Harlem, New York, in 1938. Wells became a late night hotspot for jazz

Fried chicken and waffles at Hattie's in Saratoga (*Photo by Heather Bohn-Tallman; http://hbtphoto.pass.us/hatties-brunch-1/i-gFK4c77949697 from Heather Bohm-Tallman photography, http://hbtphoto.com/; http:// hbtphoto.blogspot.com/*)

musicians, who would go after their various gigs. The musicians, arriving too late for dinner but too early for breakfast, enjoyed the appetizing compromise of fried chicken and waffles. Before long, Wells was frequented by the likes of Sammy Davis Jr. and Nat King Cole (who held his wedding reception there)."[22] Today the combination of fried chicken and waffles for brunch is served in many places around the United States including Roscoe's in California, Ella's in Florida, and at Hattie's in Upstate New York. Other popular Southern brunch dishes include crab Benedict and simple seafood omelets.

Some claim that brunch is a Southern tradition that was enjoyed after Mass and originated in New Orleans rather than New York City:

> Brunch is a New Orleans tradition born from the heart of the Catholic faith. Until the mid-twentieth century, Catholics were prohibited by church law from eating or drinking anything after midnight on Saturday, if they intended to go to Communion on Sunday morning. After Mass, those who had been fasting were hungry and ready for a meal, though in many cases it was too late for breakfast and too early for lunch. Hence brunch became a favorite Sunday meal for Catholics in New Orleans. . . . Whether it was Catholicism, the street vendors or the "second breakfast" at Madame Begue's that inspired brunch in New Orleans, the tradition continues at many restaurants of the Crescent City.[23]

In the Midwest, brunch diversity historically has been contingent on class, cultural heritage, and location. Brunch varies between the rural Midwest and cities such as Chicago and Minneapolis/St. Paul. Brunch first became popular in the Midwest in the Windy City. In Chicago, traditional brunch fare has always varied especially in terms of class. In his book *American Food: The Gastronomic Story*, Evan Jones makes the argument that because of Chicago's affluence during the Gilded Age, Chicago was one of the first places that popularized brunch. Since the 1960s, Chicago has had a well-established brunch scene from comfort food at Ann Sather's and Lou Mitchell's to high-end brunch at the Gage and formal brunches at historic hotels such as the Drake. You can also get brunch at trendy spots from the Bongo Room to Nightbird to M. Henry in Chicago. Brunch in Chicago is as diverse as brunch in New York City.

The classic brunch fare of the Midwest urban elite in the 1920s did include French-style omelets and pastries, but by the 1950s, egg casseroles and sausages had gained in popularity for Sunday brunch at home. The egg casserole is a simple dish that could be prepared ahead of time with little effort, expense, and planning. These casseroles were often prepared on Saturday evenings and consisted of white bread crumbs or crusts, eggs, milk, and often cheeses. Today we often see variations of egg casseroles from strata to simple egg bakes. Egg bakes are common in rural and small towns in the Midwest and are often served as part of Christmas brunch.[24]

Steak, eggs, and potatoes have also been classic brunch fare for many years. In discussing a family cooperative or potluck brunch, Bloch explains:

> Nothing tastes better to us than a brunch of pan-fried potatoes with golden scrambled eggs and, if the budget permits, steak. . . . One family brings the steak to be charcoal grilled out-of-doors. Another family brings rolls and a skillet of thinly sliced potatoes—parboiled and studded with finely chopped onion and a bit of green pepper—ready to finish frying at our house. We supply the beverages and have the eggs ready to be poured into the electric skillet, plugged into a porch outlet. For creamy smooth scrambled eggs, blend one second in an electric blender with seasonings and 1 teaspoon of milk for each egg.[25]

Brunch in Canada also has regional differences, and both Toronto and Montreal have their own brunch cultures. In Toronto, brunch has been around since before the 1980s largely because of established immigrant populations including Chinese and Indian immigrants, who are visible minorities in this urban center. Brunch in Toronto continues to reflect its diverse ethnic history including dim sum at Lai Wah Heen inside the Metropolitan Hotel or South Asian brunch at Lahore Tikka House. Creative types may opt for a more hipster brunch of fried chicken and waffles at the Drake or for eggs and spicy fries at Aunties and Uncles.[26] In Montreal, brunch can be French inspired including crepes and omelets. But pastries including almond croissants, financiers (a dense madeleine-like pastry) or the distinct Montreal bagel (smaller and sweeter than its New York counterpart) are often what really distinguish a Montreal brunch.

When Americans think of Mexican brunch, they often think of huevos rancheros. Brunch in Mexico has a conflicted history linked to European colonialism and indigenous food customs.[27] According to Jeffrey Pilcher, the practice of eating eggs for breakfast (and later brunch), was an import from the United States: "In searching for national counterparts to Eggs Benedict, Mexican chefs served huevos rancheros (ranch-style eggs) fried with tomato and chili sauce."[28] Mexican cuisine continues to have an influence on brunch in the Southwest and Midwest. With the recent influx of Mexican immigrants, we can find Mexican brunches even in small towns in Iowa.

Huevos rancheros (*Photo by JamesYoung; www.jamieyoungphoto.com/contact%201.html*)

BRUNCH IN GREAT BRITAIN AND WESTERN EUROPE

Although brunch was invented in England, it took a bit longer to become popular in Great Britain than in the United States. Today in England, however, we can easily find the English brunching on dippy eggs and soldiers, bubbles and squeak, or spicy omelets and curried potatoes. British brunch reflects both its English traditions and its colonial history.

Laura Mason explains:

> The breakfast-lunch combination of brunch is known in Britain, but it is regarded as a transatlantic import. It is available in some cafes, and sometimes served in private homes, but has not eroded the affection for the British breakfast and often depends on the same foods. This type of breakfast developed in the context of nineteenth-century country-house life, when a fashion for house parties developed and the idea of a large breakfast evolved. Food was kept hot over burners and everyone helped themselves. At its most extensive a meal might include items such as deviled kidneys, curry, mutton cutlets, poached fish and cold cuts of meat such as ham or tongue. It was a breakfast intended to keep people going during days of hunting or shooting in cold weather. [29]

In England, brunch remains a weekend event in hotels and restaurants. In London today we can enjoy selections of eggs Benedict, scones and clotted cream, kippers, and kedigree all on the brunch menu. Bumpkin's new English cuisine brunch menu includes salt beef hash, full English breakfast and Scottish shortbread berry pie. Black pudding (blend of onions, pork fat, oatmeal, and pig blood), scones and clotted cream, crumpets, dippy eggs (soft boiled eggs), bangers and mash (sausages and mashed potatoes), and bubbles and squeak (fried potatoes and cabbage) are just a few dishes that you may find in an English brunch. Kedigree, a dish of smoked fish (haddock, whitefish, or salmon) and rice is sometimes served for large breakfast parties or brunch. The recipe for kedigree usually includes curry powder; kedigree is based on the Indian rice and lentil dish kichree (clearly a product of colonial India).[30]

Brunch in Scotland was influenced by the English full breakfast, but in Scotland, brunch often includes some sort of combination of bangers (sausages) and potato or vegetable mash. Today you can even find vegetarian bangers and mash at the Monster Mash Café in Edinburgh. Edinburgh was quick to adapt its cuisine to both the locavare and organic trends. Eggs, black pudding (a blood-and-meat-based pudding), beans, and a potato scone often accompany bangers in a Scottish brunch. You can still order up the national Scottish dish of haggis (a meat pudding that consists of organs and oatmeal) at most restaurants, but many hotels and restaurants in Edinburgh reflect Scotland's regional and global culinary influences.

Brunch in Ireland today usually includes some combination of eggs, sausages or Irish bacon, potatoes, and soda or rye bread. Historically, soda bread can be traced back to the traditional Irish breakfast,[31] and it substitutes baking soda for yeast, making it quick to prepare. Bacon and eggs as well as oatmeal porridge have been eaten since at least the nineteenth century as part of Irish breakfast and are part of Irish modern brunches.[32] An Irish brunch for a special occasion may incorporate sausages or savory puddings as well. White pudding consists mostly of pork fat and oatmeal, and black pudding tends to consist of blood and oatmeal. The weekend brunch at Farm in Dublin includes free-range Irish sausage, O'Neil's dry-cured "old-style" bacon, organic poached egg, black and white pudding, organic breakfast mushrooms, beans, served with choices of soda bread, spelt, or rye toast.[33] Oatmeal porridge, smoked salmon, and black pudding emphasize the Irish culinary influence of the menu at the Merrion Hotel's brunch.[34]

FRANCE AND GERMANY

The French historically resisted culinary influences from outside their culture, as a mode of gastronationalism.[35] Some say there is no real brunch in France, but in a 2005 *New York Times* article, Bob Morris explored who brunches in France: "Plenty of people, to judge from local restaurants, and also (*zut alors!*) the French. In Paris recently Le Brunch has caught on in a city that always kept Sundays quiet and meals distinct. 'Est-ce que vous brunchez?' has even entered the common parlance."[36] Food writers have confirmed that "*le brunch*" has definitely caught on in Paris, and others would argue that brunch has always been in Paris as *Grand petit dejeuner*, which literally means "big small lunch" but often translates into a large breakfast or the second meal of the day. Civitello also confirms that "brunch, an American invention, caught on in France as *le brunch*."[37] French brunch is synonymous with croissants and coffee, and France, of course, can be credited with the creation of hollandaise sauce in the seventeenth century in Normandy.[38]

Many restaurants are closed on Sundays in Paris, but those that are open often include *brunch Dimanche* (Sunday brunch). The Marais district remains popular for brunching in Paris.[39] At Helmut Newcake, brunch entrees include quiches, smoked salmon, scrambled eggs, financiers, cannelés, and éclairs. Today in Paris, you can find brunch at the touristy bistros near the Eiffel Tower serving omelets and frites. But you can also brunch at Breakfast in America if you crave a greasy American brunch. Even as brunch becomes global, it is still perceived as an American tradition.

The German term *gabelfrühstück* translates as "fork breakfast," "second breakfast," or "brunch" and usually consists of some combination of traditional German sausages, mustards, and breads. While it may have previously served as more of a second breakfast, as *gabelfrühstück* was absorbed by Viennese cuisine it

Sunday brunch plate in Café Norden, Copenhagen (*Photograph by Thomas Gasienica. © Thomas Gasienica*)

transformed into more of a brunch.[40] Today in Berlin, brunch culture thrives from new Turkish-influenced diners to traditional European bistros. Café Rix in Berlin is an institution and well known for its Sunday brunch, which serves assorted sausages, Emmentaler fondue, and locally brewed beers. Weisswurst (a Bavarian white sausage) and kaiserschmarrn (Austrian pancakes) are both German foods that can be found on breakfast and brunch menus as well.

BRUNCH IN THE MEDITERRANEAN AND THE MIDDLE EAST

From France we move to more recent traditions of brunch in Turkey, where East meets West in Istanbul. Today in Istanbul brunch is found in most hotels, and is seen as a Western tradition, but like most cosmopolitan centers, hotels in Istanbul cater to tourists, upper-class natives, and transnationals. Brunch in Istanbul is largely a combination of Western meal patterns and eastern dishes.

It's only in Istanbul that you can have menemen (a spicy egg dish), gozlem (tiny Turkish pancakes), simit (a croissant-like pastry with sesame), and clotted cream in the afternoon. The most traditional brunch dish in Turkey is menemen, a dish of soft scrambled eggs cooked with spices, tomatoes, and peppers, usually served in a sahan (a copper pan with handles). It is often served at breakfast, brunch, or lunch with bread for dipping. The Middle Eastern dish shakshuka is similar but also incorporates cumin, turmeric, and other chilies, and is often served with a spicier tomato sauce. Variations of shakshuka can be found in Lebanon, Palestine, and Israel, sometimes with regional versions of the tomato sauce and often served with pita, cheeses, or labneh (yogurt dip).

If brunch is on Friday, is it still brunch? The history of brunch is tied to religion in both the West and the Middle East. In England and the United States, brunch was structured around church attendance, and similarly, brunch in the Middle East is structured around the Islamic prayer schedule, specifically Friday prayer. Friday is the holy day in Islam, centering around *zuhr* (afternoon prayer). Brunching in the Middle East grew out of the tradition of both not working on Friday and sharing a leisurely meal after Friday services. Since Thursday evening and Friday morning officially kick off the weekend, Friday has become the traditional day of brunch in the Middle East in general, and in the United Arab Emirates specifically.

Brunch in the Middle East took off by the 1990s as an indulgent weekend tradition largely practiced by expatriates, tourists, and the elite. The brunch scene in Dubai is largely based around the country's luxurious hotels. These are often champagne brunches despite Islamic restrictions on alcohol. Dubai's restaurant industry has been built on both the transnational population as well as a thriving tourist industry. In the United Arab Emirates, brunch has become quite the lavish tradition as part of hotel culture in Dubai and Doha. We also see brunch practices in Lebanon, Jordan, and Egypt. But in the Middle East in particular, brunch has become a symbol of excess and overindulgence. Since the 1990s, hotels and tourism have expanded, and especially in Dubai we have seen extravagant brunch menus develop in all the high-end hotel chains as well as some of the most elite resorts including the Ritz Carlton.

However, it is noteworthy that even though the tradition is a "Friday brunch," the Friday brunch clientele are not always Middle Eastern natives. The customers range from expatriates and tourists to the elite of Dubai society. The brunch industry is very much tied to both the tourist and entertainment industries. Many of Dubai's most famous brunch spots also include some form of entertainment, such as performers, musicians, and artists. Chadner Navarro writes about "Dubai's Outlandish Brunch Culture" for the *Huffington Post* as more over the top than what you find in New York City:

> When it comes to cities with great brunch traditions, it is hard to top New York, a place that seems to have perfected the ways in which one can eat eggs well into a leisurely afternoon. But a desert-based upstart may be looking to take over. Dubai has developed a reputation for creating some of the world's grandest buildings, water fountains and shopping malls, and its sights are now set on becoming a premier destination for the hallowed weekend repast.
>
> In this emirate, Friday brunch—workweeks here run Sunday to Thursday; Friday officially starts the weekend—has become a serious social and culinary institution. Locals and visitors alike indulge in their Champagne wishes and caviar dreams, and every eatery in the desert wonderland is commit-

ted to staging a foodie undertaking that will stand up to its closest rival.[41]

In other parts of the Middle East such as Egypt, foul mudammas (mashed beans) is often eaten with feta or manori cheese, pita, and olives for a simple brunch at home. In Lebanon, labneh and olives are staples at both breakfast and brunch. Bread with zaatar (a spice blend), foul mudammas, various dips including hummus and baba ganoush, and fried eggs with sumac would also be part of a traditional Lebanese brunch.

Brunch is a Western tradition that has spread to the Middle East and beyond as a result of globalization, immigration, transnationalism, and changes in the economy.

INDIA AND PAKISTAN

Brunch in South Asia is a result of English colonialism, globalization, and transnationalism. Breakfast had become eggs, toast, and tea in many middle- and upper-class families by the early twentieth century.[42] By the 1940s brunch had been imported from Great Britain as an English tradition, and in a second wave by the 1990s brunch returned to India as a result of immigration, educated Indians and Pakistanis working and studying abroad, and tourism from the United States. Banarji explains that breakfast as a meal was first popularized among Westernized Indians, especially those who were able to study in England and then return.[43] These breakfasts (and later brunch) often featured kulchas, a type of stuffed bread, usually filled with potatoes and spices, eaten in Punjab.[44] Brunch might not be an indigenous or authentic Indian meal, but it has been adapted by Indian and Pakistani middle- and upper-class families and often reflects a fusion of Western and Eastern culinary traditions. In India we may eat a spicy omelet or may opt for sweets such as gajar ka halwa or sheer kurma, and in South Asia, brunch continues to evolve as fusion cuisine to reflect changes in migration and globalization.

The famed Indian actress and cookbook author Madhur Jaffrey writes about the Anglo-Indian influence on breakfast and egg preparation in *From Curries to Kebabs*. She explains: "Curried hard-boiled eggs came into their own during British rule in India. Colonial Britons loved their curries and eggs in the morning and often the two were combined into one dish that was eaten with rice for both breakfast and lunch."[45] Jaffrey gives us a "hard-boiled eggs in a Delhi-style sauce" recipe and describes it as "ideal for a Sunday brunch or late supper," and eaten with "flat breads or rice."[46] She also provides a recipe for "Indian-style Curried Omelet Pie," which includes cumin, mushrooms, heavy cream, and curry powder. She explains, "I often serve this for Sunday brunch with [another of her recipes] Potatoes with Ginger."[47] Her cookbook *Indian Cooking* includes a recipe for vegetable omelets with potatoes or courgettes (zucchini), served with paratha, a flat bread, as a favorite brunch dish.[48]

Indian cookbooks also often include brunch recipes for idli (south Indian steamed rice cake), upma (south Indian salty snack), and uttapam (south Indian Salty pancake).[49] In *Indian Cooking*, Agarwal provides several recipes for Indian brunch and breakfast dishes including spicy scrambled eggs. Every Indian family had a variation of this, which at minimum includes onions, garlic, chili powder, and possibly garam masala or cilantro.[50]

In India and Pakistan, brunch at home is more common among the middle class and the educated, while brunch at restaurants and hotels remains popular among the well traveled, tourists, and the upper class.

So what is a traditional brunch in India? In India, as in the United States, brunch has great diversity and varies by region, religion, and class, but it is mostly comprised of savory dishes. In India, Sunday brunch often includes aloo puree (curried potatoes and tortillas), cholee (spicy chickpeas with potatoes and onions), and spicy omelets. Among northern Indian and Muslim Indian families, meat kebobs, including seekh kebabs, behari kebabs, and patties with naans, rotis, and puris (breads and tortillas) also can be eaten with brunch.

For South Asian Muslim families in particular, Eid brunch can be part of the festivities on Eid al-Adha. On this holiday it is *sunna* (recommended) for Muslims to fast until prayer, and then following religious services, elaborate brunches are served. Eid al-Adha brunches often include sheer kurma (vermicelli pudding), gulab jaman (sweet dumplings), or gajar ki hulwa (sweet shredded carrot pudding). These brunches are usually served and hosted in homes.

In India, brunch may be popular only among the upper class and elite, but Indian immigrants also look at brunch as a time to relax and have a day of leisure. Indians often brunch at home with their families, but brunch can also be an event for eating out. Delhi has quite a restaurant scene, with brunch options at fine dining establishments and hotels, as does Mumbai. In Mumbai, it is clear that brunch has really arrived, especially among the wealthy class, and their practice of brunching is comparable to the lavish hotel brunches in Dubai. The *Economist* recently highlighted Mumbai's lavish brunch scene:

> The age of the brunch reflects rising numbers of wealthy folk. . . . Mumbai's sports clubs, with British colonial roots, used to be the ticket. But they are now the preserve of the hereditary rich. The members' notice board of the poshest of the lot, the Willingdon Club, reads like a Who's Who of the city's industrial dynasties. For newly minted entrepreneurs and professionals, that leaves hotels and restaurants. They are anyway better for showing off. Men flash Rolexes as they reach for the dim sum. . . . The number of five-star hotels in Mumbai has risen even as the growth in foreign visitors has slowed with India's economy. Occupancy rates have fallen to 50–60%

across the city. This has led to a culinary arms race as hoteliers fight to attract locals. Sushi bars are standard. . . . Dessert counters look like Willy Wonka fantasies, with chocolate fountains and giant revolving ice-cream vats. Playing on nostalgia, most buffet spreads feature posh versions of pani-puri, a street snack that slum-dwellers buy for a few rupees. Live music is essential. Wilburn D'costa, a long-established guitarist at Indigo, a restaurant, says "Hotel California" and "Viva Las Vegas" are the favourites. It is unimaginable luxury for the millions of Mumbaikars below the poverty line. . . . Ferried about by chauffeurs and absolved from household chores by servants, they have become a corpulent race apart from their skinny compatriots. Perhaps they need to invent a new institution: the Sunday afternoon walk.[51]

From India, we can go next door to Pakistan and also see more variations on brunch. In Pakistan, breakfast

tends to be a fairly heavy affair called Halva Puri Cholay or Halva Puri for short. It consists of two separate dishes, one of halva (a sweet made from semolina) and the other Aloo Cholay (a spicy chickpea and potato curry) eaten with puri—a small round deep fried flat bread. This would usually be accompanied by lassi, which is made from yoghurt and can be salty or sweet. The sweet option is often topped with malai, a thick fresh cream. Breakfast is generally followed by Chai—a black tea with milk. In urban areas and cities the Western influence means that eggs and toast with butter and jam are becoming ever more popular.[52]

Despite being a predominantly Muslim country, brunch in Pakistan is also on Sunday—another effect of British colonization. In Pakistan, brunch often includes meat dishes such as kebabs and meat curries alongside naans (breads) and spicy cholles (chickpeas) and potatoes. Tea or chai is often favored over coffee as the caffeinated drink of choice. Lassis, which are yogurt-based drinks, are also popular daytime and brunch drinks. In particular, mango and other fresh fruit lassis have always been traditional Indian and Pakistani breakfast and brunch drinks.

KOREA, CHINA, AND DIM SUM

Su Hyun Lee explains that by 2007, brunch in South Korea had become popular among Koreans who had worked abroad in the United States:

> What makes the brunch fashion somewhat surprising is that Koreans tend to be reluctant to try non-Korean foods. Even when traveling abroad, they gravitate toward kimchi (fermented vegetables) and bibimpap (rice with vegetables and chili paste). Eating steak and potatoes with knives and forks can be considered an act of sophistication.
>
> Brunch is popular even though some Koreans do not really like the food served at the meal: eggs and bacon, pancakes and toast are all a marked contrast to the usual Korean breakfast of rice, soup and vegetables. The portions are huge by Korean standards. And brunch can be expensive, typically around 25,000 won, or $27.50.[53]

This is a clear example of how globalization contributes to shaping brunch patterns outside the West. However, in the last two decades, this practice has gone full circle as the United States has been incorporating other ethnic and cultural innovations into its own brunch practices. A key example of this is dim sum.

We could make the case that brunch actually has always existed in China through the practice of dim sum. Dim sum is a traditional midday meal composed of small plates of sweet and savory steamed or fried dishes. The term *dim sum* means "touch the heart" and is often linked to *Yum cha*, or teatime. The history of dim sum can be traced back to the Cantonese in the tenth century when travelers would stop for small meals and tea: "People took the snacks their hearts desired from carts rolled around all day in tea houses. Habituées of tea houses ate dim sum to socialize. Businessmen liked to negotiate deals over dim sum. . . . Almost all the early immigrants came from Canton. . . . Usually the chefs steam or fry the dumplings filled with fish, shellfish, meat, fowl or vegetables or blends of several ingredients. . . . With the dumplings, you eat stir-fried noodles or soup."[54]

In Hong Kong, dim sum is prevalent, but tourists often stick to the most popular dim sum dishes.[55] Har gow is one of the most popular dumpling dishes in Hong Kong and is usually made with either shrimp or lobster. Siu mai is a meatball dumpling usually made with pork. Cha siu bao is a dumpling made of Chinese buns but steamed in a bamboo basket. It is a sweet dumpling often eaten at the end of a meal. "Phoenix talons" are the traditional dim sum of chicken feet. Cheung fun is a rice dish made of steamed rice noodles but often served with meat or vegetables inside.

Traditionally, dim sum is more of a snack in China, but it became a popular meal in the United States, especially in California and New York City, where Chinese food grew in popularity by the 1970s. Sundays tend to be the busiest day for going out for dim sum, which has contributed to the practice becoming such a popular brunch option in the United States. A 2012 *Saveur* article discusses dim sum as a new American brunch tradition: "Going out for Chinese dim sum is one of our favorite brunch excursions—the clatter of the carts, the endless plates of dumplings and steamed buns—but sometimes a leisurely morning in your own kitchen is what beckons most. Have the best of both worlds with this brunch menu of shrimp dumplings, pork bao, fresh spring rolls, and more."[56] *Saveur*'s sample brunch menu includes boiled chicken dumplings, bao, fresh rice sheets with shrimp, fresh spring rolls, soup dumplings, pork and chive dumplings, shrimp and pea shoot dumplings, pork pot stickers, Chinese broccoli, and green tea.

Brunch around the world varies between cultures, but it is still a leisurely weekend tradition. From the extravagant Friday brunches in New York, Mumbai, and Dubai to the more relaxed brunches in Mexico City or Paris, we can see why this tradition is so attractive. Brunch has traveled from England to the United States and India, from the United States to Mexico and Dubai. Brunch is diverse in its beginnings, and brunch is diverse today in its offerings. For many of us it's a time to experiment with ethnic recipes or sample exotic cuisines. Brunch can even make some of us culinary adventurers.[57]

3

BRUNCH AT HOME

Why bother to do research on the trendiest brunch spots, attempt to make brunch reservations, or wait over an hour for brunch, when you can have brunch at home? Brunch at home can be very different than brunch out, since the host or hostess sets the menu, the pace, and the level of formality. Hosting a brunch in the home historically has adapted to changes in cultural and social norms. Brunch at home tends to be an informal affair today but began as the elegant breakfast party in the 1920s.

The *Huffington Post* recently explained:

> As people who complain about brunch will usually tell you, it's a way for restaurants to use up ingredients that have been sitting around, give their weakest link line cooks some hours and generally sling overpriced eggs and mimosas into your face. Brunch at home, however, is completely the opposite. When you make brunch for yourself and your friends, you are pointedly taking time out to do something really special. Dinner parties are special, but we all eat dinner. When you invite friends over for brunch, you are automatically making their day more luxurious by making sure they eat something amazing right away, not just another bowl of granola.[1]

Brunch at home often conjures up images of Christmas or Easter brunch with families, or close friends on a leisurely late morning or Sunday afternoon. Brunch traditionally marked holidays and occasions such as Mother's Day, Father's Day, and bridal brunches. These brunches tend to be family meals prepared in the house on Sunday. More recently, brunch has become a weekend meal served Saturday or Sunday to mark baby showers, birthdays, and even family reunions. Brunch at home is an excuse to relax, indulge, and socialize by sharing comfort foods, often with decadent pastries or cocktails.

The history of brunch at hom can be traced to 1889, when breakfast parties were suggested as an inexpensive way to entertain in Mary Henderson's *Practical Cooking and Giving*.[2] Brunching at home is a tradition we can trace back to the 1930s

Baked eggs in 1942 (Photo by Ann Rosener; http://lcweb2.loc.gov/ service/pnp/fsa/8b07000/8b07600/8b07647v.jpg)

when upper-class women saw it as an easy way to entertain after breakfast parties had become a common way to entertain in the 1920s. Lunch parties, which had become popular by the 1950s, had historically been women's events often thrown on weekdays, but breakfast parties included men and women and were often elite social gatherings on weekends. In many ways, these parties at home were marked by class, gender, and cultural norms. Brunch, naturally, was a combination of both, as brunch parties began as Sunday late-afternoon gatherings. The earliest brunch parties were often bridal brunches with men and women in attendance and later became more gendered occasions. Brunch parties at home became ways to mark baby showers, bridal showers, and almost any occasion.

We first see brunch at home mentioned in the society pages of newspapers in the 1930s and 1940s. By the 1950s, brunch was often perceived as a time saver for both the housewife and the working woman. Secondly, brunch-like breakfast was often seen as economical, as it often was based on a few basic ingredients including coffee, eggs, and breads.

In 1954, James Beard explained that with brunch "you can serve what you want, whenever you want—just be sure you give your guests an eye-opener or two before serving."[3] Beard also reinforced the idea that brunch is a meal with no rules, and no established menu:

> Brunch is an ideal and rewarding way for the busy person to entertain. You are not bound by any specific rules in planning your menus. There is a great elasticity in the hour for which you decide to invite you guests—it can be anywhere from ten-thirty in the morning till one-thirty in the afternoon. It depends largely upon what hour the sleepy hosts choose to arise and start the preparations. Drinks are not necessary, yet they're certainly a pleasant start to brunch. But they should be something different—eye openers as well as stimulants. Therefore drinks with a good deal of fruit—Bloody Mary's,

Golden Screws, Daiquiris or just the old favorite iced French
Champagne—are the type of drinks which most appeal to
guests at an early hour. And be sure to have pots of coffee and
tea at hand, for those who prefer that type of stimulant rather
than the alcoholic variety. And don't serve too many drinks
before this meal, which is, for many the first of the day.
Brunch is a strictly informal meal. Be casual and use your
pleasantest china, glass and linens. Don't try to be formal. If
you have a large kitchen, set up a serving buffet there and let
guests come to the kitchen for their food. This is especially
good when you cook omelets or egg dishes which should be
served at once rather than allowed to cool in a serving dish on
your dining room table. Or, if you serve at a table, have everything prepared at once and let guests help themselves or serve
them from your seat as host. Don't hurry anyone and have
plenty of munchy food that can be eaten with "post-meal" cups
of coffee and tea when the good rich conversation begins to
flow. It's a rest day. Relax.[4]

OCCASIONS FOR BRUNCH

Holidays

Brunch eventually became a way to mark celebrations and holidays, from Easter and bridal brunches that first became popular
in the 1940s to more recently Father's Day and grandparent
brunches. Brunch today is often served for no occasion at all, but
it can still be a way to celebrate religious holidays, weddings, and
other special occasions. The history of Easter and Christmas
brunches at home in the United States can be traced back to the
1930s.

Easter and Christmas brunches were a time to share a family
meal after a religious service, but today they are often part of a
holiday weekend and do not necessarily follow religious services.
Easter brunches, like lunches, have often been based around a

roast, lamb, or carved meat dish followed by pies, pastries, and Easter egg hunts. Christmas brunches varied but were usually served on Christmas Day, often after opening Christmas presents. They vary in formality and dishes.

Easter Sunday may be the most popular holiday for brunch at home. In 1966, Craig Claiborne, the food writer for the *New York Times Magazine*, proclaimed that Easter Sunday is the ideal time for a Sunday brunch, and eggs Benedict is the ideal brunch dish: "There is no Sunday more suited to brunch than Easter. . . . And thought for thought, there isn't a dish more suited to brunch than eggs Benedict, a dish with a hundred variations. It may be with a base of Dutch Rusk or English muffin, with bacon or ham hollandaise sauce Mornay, but the most glorious of all is eggs on brioche Benedict."[5]

Easter brunch also lent itself to coloring Easter eggs, egg hunts, and even cooperative get-togethers such as a "progressive Easter brunch." In 1954, in *Sunset* magazine the authors suggest a progressive Easter brunch and egg hunt: "Here's an Easter brunch that can be fun for everyone—toddlers, teen-agers, and adults. Our suggestion is a progressive egg hunt and brunch for a group of families who live in the same neighborhood, know each other well, and like to do things together. This Easter get-together, right after Sunday school or church, will be more easily handled if the hunt and brunch are limited to three homes, and with any additional family groups cooperating on coloring and hiding the eggs."[6] Easter brunch was also still associated with church attendance in the 1950s, and Easter egg hunts were often an integral part of the Easter brunch.

Bridal Brunch

Bridal brunches are also part of the history of brunching at home. The wedding brunch at home began as bridal breakfast parties of the elite during the gilded age. But even today bridal brunches remain popular because this is often a time for the extended family or out-of-town wedding guests to come together. Bridal brunches are usually thrown the day after the wedding, before the couple leaves for their honeymoon. This brunch is usually hosted by close family members who live in the city of the wedding ceremony and historically was thrown by the parents of the bride or groom. The wedding breakfast was also a tradition, but between the 1930s and 1950s we began to see the bridal brunch as an alternative to a traditional breakfast. In 1938, in the *San Antonio Light* advises, "A wedding breakfast may be served at any morning hour as late as 1:00 pm. Since it is seldom as early an event as the routine breakfast, the hostess is wise to plan a substantial meal. In fact most wedding breakfasts . . . are called brunches. The attractive plate of orange segments and strawberries surrounding a mound of powdered sugar is an excellent first course for the wedding brunch."[7]

Early wedding brunches did lend themselves to more formal affairs complete with floral arrangements, table settings, and several courses. As early as 1942 Emily Post began to acknowledge the changing patterns of meals from breakfast to brunch in "Good Taste Today":

> Dear Mrs. Post: What is a brunch? I am told it is a new and fashionable variety of entertainment.
>
> Mrs. Post: To me the word brunch is the unpleasantly crippled combination of the words breakfast and lunch. . . . It is a twelve o'clock breakfast; it has always been fashionable especially in the hunting community. But why a hunt breakfast (or a wedding breakfast) should suddenly be called a hunt brunch or a wedding brunch is more than I can understand. Perhaps now that coffee is unattainable and big breakfast cups of it will be very hard to provide, the word "brunch" will be sent bunching back to the limbo whence it came![8]

Emily Post was not pleased with the invention or spread of brunch initially. Her comments indicated severe disapproval as if to suggest brunch was an improper meal with no real tradition or etiquette.

In recent decades the bridal brunch at home has become more casual. The bridal brunch provides an opportunity for bridal families to share a meal and spend some time together before the bridal couple leaves for their honeymoon, often including out-of-town guests also. If the opening of wedding gifts is a part of the bridal weekend, gifts are often opened at the bridal brunch with close family in attendance.

Regardless of the level of formality, the bridal brunch at home is a ritual in American families that often ends the wedding weekend. It is a time for the couple to spend a few hours with family and out-of-town guests, share a casual meal, and open presents. The structure of the bridal brunch at home can vary, but in recent decades it has become a part of the traditional middle-class wedding weekend.

Casual and Convenience Brunches

In 1967, in *Betty Crocker's Hostess Cookbook*, the authors explain:

> A party at midday offers a change of pace from evening entertaining, and a brunch or lunch has charms quite different from those of a dinner party. Brunch, as the name implies, is a combination of breakfast and lunch and may be served any time between ten or ten-thirty and one o'clock. A weekday brunch may precede a committee meeting or any feminine business, even shopping, but probably the most popular brunches are co-ed affairs served late on Sunday morning. Borrow an idea from fine restaurants and offer each guest a cup of coffee the minute he arrives. Serve English-style from a sideboard and let everyone help himself from a chafing dishes

or platters on a hot tray. If you like you can provide some lazy after-eating entertainment. Buy three or four Sunday papers and set them out for browsing. Have a giant jigsaw puzzle ready for assembling. Encourage your guests to do as they please. Some may want to listen to records, some may favor a walk, and still others may prefer to work on the crossword puzzle.[9]

Betty Crocker emphasizes brunch as a coed affair but by the 1990s brunch took on a more feminine association. Women tend to host brunch parties or go out for brunch more than men; brunch recipes and features are often aimed at all female guests unless they are marking a religious holiday or celebration. Casual brunches are ways for women to socialize in the same way that lunch parties in the home were a way for women to get together. Betty Crocker introduced brunch to many American wives, but also helped popularize the brunch casserole, the idea of a themed brunch, and the pancake party.

The brunch casserole was an easy brunch dish incorporating eggs, bread, and bacon into one simple dish. In many ways the brunch casserole symbolizes a casual and informal brunch of ease, while eggs Benedict indicates a more refined brunch. The Betty Crocker editors explain that "the egg casserole is rich with cheese and bits of mushroom, crusted with caraway rye bread. The bacon in crispy curls makes a delightful garnish. And the coffee cake becomes a full-scale dessert with the addition of a sweet-tart lemon sauce."[10] The other popular option suggested is the pancake party: "If your brunch guests include men or children or both, your reputation is bound to be enhanced by a do-it-yourself flapjack buffet. Offer at least three variations of pancakes and waffles, with one sweet and one meat topper for the pancakes and one special ingredient for the waffles. Bring on the bacon, coffee and milk. Voila! Your own pancake house."[11]

Brunch casseroles, cheese bakes, waffle stations, and pancake parties were all ways to host a casual brunch, but convenience foods provided more options for preparing a quick and simple brunch. In 1951's *The Can-Opener Cookbook*, Poppy Cannon introduced women to innovative but simple methods for creating home-cooked meals using prepared foods, including canned foods.[12] Poppy Cannon's hollandaise sauce recipe was often re-printed as part of her "Graceful Viennese Brunch."[13] But it was in the 1950s through the use of convenience foods that brunch really took on its informal and casual setting.

Susannah Blake explains that "weekends, vacations, sleep-overs and house-parties provide the perfect excuse for blurring the boundaries between breakfast and lunch. The socializing opportunities at breakfast or brunch get-together offers are second-

Waffles at home (*Photo by Lesley Procelli; http://uglybutgood.files.wordpress.com/2013/08/p1000686.jpg***)**

to-none: the atmosphere is decidedly relaxed and informal, and its timing allows everyone to head off to different activities satiated and energized, and still with much of the day free."[14]

Convenience food along with the crunch that women felt in terms of time and money in the 1950s helped increase the popularity of casual brunches. Convenience food continued to play a role in the menus for brunch at home from the 1950s until the present. Aunt Jemima, Jimmy Dean, Duncan Hines, and Bisquick all make staple products for breakfast, but we often use them in combination with dishes made from scratch to create leisurely brunch menus at home. Pillsbury crescent rolls might accompany a homemade quiche and Jimmy Dean sausage. Duncan Hines muffins might be the sweet treat at the end of a brunch of corned beef hash and eggs. Bisquick biscuits or pancakes could be the basis of a sweet or savory brunch served with bacon, maple syrup, and scrambled eggs. Breakfast pastries and breads are often made from mixes or frozen dough or are picked up from supermarkets. Making breads and pastries can be time consuming and many Americans continue to use mixes or frozen dough, especially for their brunch sweet offerings. However, in the last five years we've seen a trend toward a new domesticity, especially with middle-class women returning to "authentic" homemade recipes and relying on organic and local ingredients.[15]

Casual Sunday brunches not only lent themselves to convenience foods but also to combining breakfast and lunch and reducing household labor and the time involved in preparing meals. A typical casual brunch could include a baked egg dish; Pillsbury cinnamon buns; fruit salad; and coffee, tea, and fruit juice. These conveniences allowed for variety and the increased popularity of semi-homemade meals. The informality of brunch also made it easier to brunch more often at home and include men and families for brunch at home.

Blueberry pancakes (*Photo by James Young; www.jamieyoungphoto.com/contact%201.html*)

SETTING AND BRUNCH ETIQUETTE

In 1955, the Culinary Arts Institute published a guide to serving breakfast and brunch in which they explained some of the social norms for serving brunch at home: "Brunch is neither breakfast nor lunch, but a delightful combination of both. It is served any time before one o'clock. Brunch, served early, generally means simple breakfast foods. Served later, the menu may be an expanded and more elaborate breakfast, possibly served buffet style. Or it may more closely resemble a luncheon, although soups and salads seldom are on the menu and the dessert, if any, is light, such as fruit or cookies."[16]

Until the 1970s, cookbook authors and etiquette guides suggested that brunch time at home ended at 1 PM. The earlier the brunch the more simple the menu, was a rule of thumb that indicated that the later the brunch, the more preparation was involved.

The setting for brunch at home is often dictated by the occasion. Bridal brunches or Christmas brunches can be more formal. Father's Day or Mother's Day brunches can be more casual. The dexterity of brunch is also what makes it so popular. It can be themed, formal or casual, large or intimate. Brunch can be served as a buffet or with place settings.

In the 1970s, Pat Jester explained:

> Because brunch is considered a special occasion, it isn't a true brunch unless some thought and care have gone into the planning and preparation. Planning a brunch menu is no different from planning any other menu. The basic guidelines remain the same. Here are a few to get you started. A well-rounded brunch should start with a beverage, such as a punch or fruit juice, and an appetizer or soup. If you want to serve appetizers, any hors d'oeuvres is appropriate. This can be followed by a light soup or by the main dish, or if you prefer, the soup can take the place of the appetizer. The main dish can vary based on the size of your group. An egg based dish such as a quiche, omelet or soufflé is always a brunch treat.[17]

Jester also explains that what makes brunch unique is that it combines the best of breakfast and lunch.

> Many of us don't enjoy the first meal of the day. It comes too soon and we aren't awake enough to prepare it or appreciate it. This is not true of brunch. By the time brunch is served, everyone is awake and at their sociable best. Brunch is usually served between the hours of 10 o'clock and 1 o'clock. It may follow church, precede a noon meeting or climax a morning of skiing or tennis. The fact that there are no rules for brunches has endeared them to everyone who enjoys cooking and entertaining. . . . The emphasis on brunch is fine food. That's what everyone will expect.[18]

The authors of *Real Simple* suggest that there is no one way to set the table for a Sunday brunch buffet but they recommend:

> Place a stack of plates at one end of the buffet table so that guests pick them up first. Choose plates with some heft (avoid flimsy paper ones) and a substantial lip: Food will be less likely to slide off. Use the Buffet Flow Chart as a guide when entertaining large groups. The food comes next. Arrange it at various heights so that guests can see and reach everything with ease. Shallow bowls and basic platters are the most user-friendly choices. . . . Use sleek flatware, as more decorative styles are often too bulky to roll up neatly. Position drinks and easy-to-grip stackable tumblers at the end of the buffet table.[19]

Rachel White in the *Huffington Post* suggests the following table settings and floral arrangements for a spring brunch:

> Since we are heading toward growing season, small potted plants like herbs and daisies are a nice idea for table decor. Choose four or five small pots to put in the center of a long table, or, depending on the number of guests you have, use them as place settings that each person can take home. Another idea is to have one stunning arrangement of tulips or another spring flower as the focal point. If you stick to one color and type of flower, the arrangement will be dramatic yet simple. If flowers are not your thing, there are some great DIY decoration ideas like these tissue paper pom-poms, or these cupcake liner garlands. No matter where you live, it is easy to bring a little spring to the table. So enjoy the sunshine or make the most of the rainy Sunday by using these hosting tips for your next brunch![20]

The food writers at Ifood.tv also explain that

> there is no proper rule on table setting for brunch. Mostly it depends on the foods you are serving. Buffet style serving is the most preferred choice for hosting the brunch. Selecting a theme can help you in deciding on the table décor. However,

it would be better to keep the decoration as . . . simple as possible. As you have to present several choices of food, any intricate decoration might get overwritten. A large centerpiece can be used as the attractive eye-catcher of the brunch table. The long-stemmed flowers or a large fruit basket or carved vegetable artwork can be the best choice for the brunch table setting. Depending on the style of serving and the type of foods, the item list will vary. If you are serving the brunch on buffet style, then follow the guidelines on setting up a buffet table. If you plan to serve the brunch on table, then choose the main dinnerware, silverware and glassware used for serving lunch. However, . . . [one] addition could be a tea or coffee set, in case you serve tea or coffee in the brunch. If you plan to serve champagne or wine, then you need to place the champagne flute or wine glass along with the tumbler.

But for a basic brunch table setting, the authors suggest: "In case of a buffet, keep the plates in a stack at the beginning. Place the side dishes, followed by the main dish and other choices. End with the essential silverware items to handle food."[21]

Most importantly, brunch at home is a time to relax or indulge with friends or family, often in the comfort of your own home. Therefore, brunch at home rarely begins before 10 AM and can linger as late 3 PM. Susan Spungen explains that brunch at home should offer sweet and savory options, but can still remain simple:

Brunch at home is very different from brunch out. It's great to cover sweet and savory tastes, but there's just too much going on here. If you want to make pancakes, let the egg dish be a simple one, such as scrambled eggs with some herbs. (And of course most people want bacon with that.) If the eggs play the starring role and you want them to be more substantial, a frittata or quiche will make your life a lot more easier than individual omelets for each guest. Even if omelets are your specialty, take into consideration the difficulty of timing. Individual eggs with ramekins are another solution. They can be assembled just before your guests arrive and then popped into the oven all at once. A fruit salad at the end of the meal will round it out perfectly.[22]

BRUNCH AT THE WHITE HOUSE

Brunch at home can also be a special occasion for even the president of the United States. The most significant brunch that the president hosts is the Easter brunch at the White House. The Easter egg roll is part of the Easter tradition at the White House and is traced back to 1878 with President Rutherford B. Hayes.

Randy James of *Time* magazine summarizes the history of the Easter egg roll:

> The daylong celebration transforms the presidential yard into official Washington's version of an amusement park, with food, games, music, storytelling, and, yes, thousands of eggs. The President and first lady generally attend, along with other notables. . . . And, of course, there is egg rolling—a European custom of murky origin wherein a hard-boiled egg is pushed, dragged, flung or otherwise propelled across a lawn with a long-handled spoon. Every child leaves with a wooden souvenir egg bearing the printed signatures of the day's hosts, the President and first lady. Washington's young people used to gather on the Capitol grounds for Easter Egg rolling in the 19th century, but lawmakers grew so peeved at the damage to the grass that in 1876 they passed the Turf Protection Law banning the practice. Bad weather nixed egg rolling the following year, but in 1878 President Rutherford B. Hayes opened the White House grounds to the displaced youngsters and a tradition began. It has continued steadily ever since, interrupted only by inclement weather and hiatuses during World Wars I and II. . . . More than 100 same-sex couples showed up at the event in 2006 with their children in an organized effort to show President Bush "that gay families exist in this country," in the words of one organizer; critics accused them of "crashing" the event. The Obamas specifically wel-

comed gay families this year, distributing tickets directly to gay rights organizations. Another innovation of the Obamas: this year's souvenir egg is designed to be environmentally friendly, using vegetable oil-based ink and wood from "sustainably managed forests. Also for the first time, tickets to this year's event were distributed over the Internet rather than via the first-come, first-served.[23]

First Lady Pat Nixon's staff arranged the first—and last—Easter egg hunt with actual eggs. In 1993, the Clintons scaled back the fanfare so that children would remember the day for its egg rolling games. A generation earlier, First Lady Pat Nixon gave out certificates of participation as a souvenir to egg rollers. Betty Ford and Rosalynn Carter distributed plastic eggs with printed notes inside from the First Lady. In 1981, President and Mrs. Ronald Reagan hosted a hunt for wooden eggs that bore the signatures of famous people. Wooden eggs soon became the official White House egg roll keepsakes. The eggs are designed to reflect the special theme of each year's event, and are inscribed with the signatures of the president and first lady. Each child under the age of twelve is given one as he or she exits the South Lawn gates.[24]

The Easter egg roll is just one significant part of the Easter brunch tradition at the White House. The actual menu of the brunch often is also noteworthy, and tends to be traditional including both sweet and savory courses. The 2008 menu for the Easter brunch was honey baked ham with maple mustard sauce, eggs Benedict, bacon, biscuits, spinach salad, waffles, sautéed asparagus, cheese grits, fresh fruit platter, double-coconut layer cake, and lemon curd trifle with fresh berries.[25]

Tammy Haddad hosts the White House Correspondent's brunch, which might be the second-most-well-known brunch in the capital. It is an annual tradition recently marking its twentieth anniversary, which can be traced back to 1993.[26] The White

House Correspondents Dinner in May of each year starts off with the Saturday Garden Brunch. This brunch is often a celebrity, star-studded affair. The White House Correspondents Association's Annual Dinner had its ninety-ninth anniversary while the Annual Garden Brunch celebrated its twentieth anniversary. "Originally held at the Palisades home of Haddad Media CEO and veteran Washington TV executive Tammy Haddad, the brunch has since moved to the historic Beall-Washington House in Georgetown. Over the years the brunch has been co-presented and honored such prestigious organizations like CURE epilepsy, The White Ribbon Foundation, and this year The Miss America Foundation. The brunch provides the first time that many new faces for Correspondents' Weekend meet their dinner sponsors."[27]

CLASSIC BRUNCH COOKBOOKS

When I imagine a brunch at home, I hope for coffee, a fresh salad, a savory egg dish, and a sweet (high-carbohydrate) pastry ending. But preparing brunch at home means relying on recipes, especially when we're hoping to elevate brunch from an everyday breakfast meal to mark a special occasion or celebration. Brunch recipes and menus are often from brunch cookbooks that started to become popular by the 1950s. But brunch recipes also come from family traditions passed on from one generation to another either orally or through community and church cookbooks.

One of the earliest brunch cookbooks was published in 1942 as *The Breakfast and Brunch Cook Book* by the Chicago Culinary Arts Institute. Its editor, Ruth Berolzheimer, explains the significance of brunch: "Brunch is the ingenious word that means a combination meal too late for breakfast and too early for lunch. Brunches follow the breakfast pattern of fruit or fruit juices, eggs, cheese, fish or meat, potatoes, breads, quick breads, and beverages, but use them in luncheon form. . . . Brunch offers really substantial fare, when you have a thick slice of ham broiled crisp at the edges."[28] This early brunch cookbook explains the pattern of dishes to be served during brunch starting with fruit juices and eggs and ending with breads and beverages. Beverages in the 1940s included both caffeinated drinks and fruit cocktails during brunch. The authors also explain that seasonal and occasional brunches are also ways to entertain at home.

For seasonal brunches recipes included almond coffee puffs, corn soufflé, honey butter, pan-broiled liver, eggs à la Benedictine, kidney veal chops, fried scallops, fruit cup, and Swedish coffee ring. "When brunch comes nearer noon than nine, a scalloped vegetable dish will be very welcome."[29] In the 1940s to 1950s especially, brunch often incorporated lunch dishes especially when brunch is served close to lunch time.

For Sunday brunches, recipes included lemon coffee cake, fresh fruit in pineapple boats, broiled lamb kidneys, puffed potatoes, rum babas, squabs en casserole, prune coffee cake, Armenian eggplant, poached eggs, strawberry coffee cake, oysters à la king, honey egg milk shake, and cornmeal griddlecakes.

Brunches that vary by region were referred to as "sectional brunches." Southern brunches might have fruited sausages with hominy, fried apples, American fried potatoes, and mint grapefruit. Midwest brunches include applesauce torte, creamed dried beef, toast timbales, and cinnamon rolls. Western brunches serve baked trout and a fruit plate. Holiday brunches include New Year's Day, St. Valentine's Day, Washington's Birthday, St. Patrick's Day, May Day, Memorial Day, Fourth of July, Labor Day and Armistice Day.[30]

After *The Breakfast and Brunch Cookbook* was published in 1942, in 1954, the Culinary Arts Institute published *Brunch, Breakfast and Morning Coffee*, in which the authors explain that "brunch is neither breakfast nor lunch, but a delightful combination of both. It is served any time before one o'clock. Brunch, served early, generally means simple breakfast foods. Served later, the menu may be an expanded and more elaborate breakfast, possibly served buffet style. Or it may more closely resemble a luncheon, although soups and salads seldom are on the menu and the dessert, if any, is light, such as fruit or cookies."[31]

The Nabisco Biscuit Company published *Late Breakfast or Brunch* in 1968, which provided menus for brunches of many occasions. A skiers' brunch, a barbecue brunch, and a football brunch are all types of brunches suggested in this cookbook. The Junior Service League published *Brunch 'n Luncheon Menus* in 1968.

By the 1970s, brunch cookbooks became more visible in American culture. The brunch meal had spread from the elite in the 1920s to the middle class by the 1950s, and brunch had become an established institution as well as a way to easily entertain at home. In particular, brunch lent itself to a diversity of occasions, dishes, preparation style, and often time- and money-saving techniques.

In *Better Homes and Gardens' Brunches and Lunches: America's Best-Loved Community Cookbook Recipes*, Christopher Cavanaugh explains:

> How sweet it is . . . waking up to a fragrant goody, fresh from the oven. Tender breads, muffins, coffee cakes, buns and buckles are all represented in this mouthwatering array of brunch time delicacies. Tempt your family with irresistibly wholesome Morning Glory Muffins, bursting with carrots, apples or nut, or lure them to the table with Cinnamon-Raisin Oatmeal Bread. Having friends to brunch? Try these eye-openers: Stuffed French Toast, Southern-style Bourbon Pecan Bread, or traditional Hot Cross Buns. From fun-to-pull apart Bubble bread to luscious Peach Coffee Cake, we'll help you free the day in culinary style.[32]

Martha Stewart, Julia Child, and even Williams and Sonoma all have popular brunch cookbooks. More recently Manhattan restaurants at the center of the New York City brunch scene have also produced numerous brunch books, including *Five Points* brunch book, *Sarabeths* cookbook, *Bubby's Brunch, Gale Gand's Brunch*, and *Clinton Street Bakery* that could be the foundation for a brunch at home. Most brunch cookbooks have chapters dedicated to egg dishes, griddle dishes, and baked breads or pastries. Brunch cookbooks also include brunch cocktails such as *Peter Joseph's Boozy Brunch*.

TRADITIONAL BRUNCH AT HOME

In *Good Mornings: Great Breakfasts and Brunches for Starting the Day Right* Michael McLaughlin explains why brunch is more special than breakfast, and most importantly, that brunch is a meal shared with others and always includes at least one dish that is extraordinary:

> Breakfast is Tuesday; brunch is Sunday. Breakfast is pancakes; brunch is crepes. Breakfast is orange juice; brunch is a screwdriver. Breakfast is Doonesbury, Cathy, and Dilbert; Brunch is Vivaldi, Sinatra, and Marian McPartland. Breakfast can be solitary, brunch requires a crowd. Brunch is breakfast with a shave. Actually there is some mostly one-way crossover. Breakfast items may appear at brunch but brunch dishes almost never show up at breakfast. Breakfast is a meal, but brunch is more a state of mind (I've served it at four in the afternoon), and as long as it feels celebratory, even if the menu is bacon, eggs, hash browns, and coffee, without a drop of champagne in sight, it's brunch. That said some things still don't belong (this list is probably personal), which is why chili, pizza, and leg of lamb are missing from the following six chapters, while little grilled steaks, gruyere fondue, and brownies are included.[33]

Whatever you decide to prepare for brunch at home, it should convey either comfort or decadence. We may leave eggs Benedict and other more tedious brunch dishes for brunch out, but brunch at home almost always includes savory egg dishes and breakfast meats, often with a sweet ending. Fresh baked breads, rolls, croissants, juices, teas, and coffee often accompany brunch. A well-rounded brunch includes savory and sweet options, even in the home. Popular savory options for brunch often include omelets, corned beef hash and eggs, quiches, roasted meats, breakfast potatoes, and breakfast meats.

But a brunch even at home does not seem quite complete without a small dessert. Sweet endings served at home can include pastries, baked desserts, or dessert bars. Sweets at brunch often include pancakes, French toast, and waffles as well. Traditional sweet brunch dishes are often the main dish but at home can serve as a supplement. Sweet brunch dishes can also be dessert pastries such as croissants, donuts, and Danishes. These can vary by family tradition and background. But many of these are often store bought as well.

Brunch offerings often depend on the occasion and how many people you are entertaining.

Brunch at home also is often an excuse to indulge in a decadent caffeine, fruit, or alcoholic drink. Brunch at home can include brunch cocktails, punches, coffees, teas, and/or simple fruit juices. But coffee or tea is necessary for any meal that begins before noon. And most guests would probably appreciate a fruity or cocktail option, especially if the brunch is at a leisurely pace and may go into the afternoon.

Coffee drinks at home can be simple and casual, either by setting up a coffee station with a fresh brewed pot of coffee or serving individual espresso drinks for a smaller more intimate brunch at home. Coffee drinks also can easily turn into adult coffee cocktails with the addition of Bailey's Irish cream. But brunch cocktails are a category of their own, including Bloody Marys, mimosas, and Bellinis. Coffee stations can have cocoas and selections of teas as well.

Brunch at home can often be a much more pleasant and relaxing affair than brunch out. It depends on the dishes and the company. Guests often expect a combination of savory and sweet, pleasant conversation, and some caffeinated beverages and a brunch cocktail (or two). But most important to a brunch at home is to not have the hurried sense of a brunch out! Brunch at home has no rules or schedule.

4

BRUNCH AWAY FROM HOME

"The luncheon or lunch but not brunch! advised Emily Post. It took her only ten lines to dismiss the custom as a 'single-headed, double-bodied deformity of the language' that 'suggests standees' at a lunch counter but not the beauty of hospitable living."[1] Like most Americans, Emily Post did embrace the brunch tradition by the 1950s. When we think of brunching out, we imagine lobster Benny, crème brûlée, French toast, and baskets of decadent pastries accompanied by espresso drinks and brunch cocktails. Brunch in itself is a special meal that many indulge in only on holidays or special occasions, but brunch out is extra special, as it allows us to savor the special dishes that we would never make for ourselves.

New York Magazine food critic Gael Greene wrote of brunch as one of life's great pleasures in her chapter, "The Beatitude of Brunch" in 1971. Greene wrote of brunch at the Plaza as an example of New York's "glamour":

> Sunday is a tender day. Fiercely fragile. Sunday is like Christmas ripe with promise; in disappointment, quite devastating. Some Sundays are not to be tested. . . . My fantasy New York is ragged and riddled by reality's blows. Yet I cling to the shreds. . . . The coffee is the best American coffee I've had in a

New York restaurant . . . cup after cup poured promptly by the waiter without reminder. . . . The $5.24 brunch—from 11 am to 2:15 pm—is proper and uptight, not even a little bit rash: poached eggs Benedict, "creamed white of chicken on toast," scrambled eggs with bacon, sausages, or ham, an aristocratic corned beef hash, and a weekly specialty—sweetbreads in a pastry tuffet, supposedly "financiere" but minus the classic quenelle, olive and truffle garnish. All first-rate except for a slightly tepid hollandaise. But how ungenteel to receive the check unbidden.[2]

New York Times critic William Grimes explains that in New York City, brunch is the most anticipated meal of the week to eat out. In "At Brunch, the More Bizarre the Better," he confirms that by the 1990s, brunching out had become a well-established brunch tradition:

When the weekend arrives and the city's daytime motor shifts into idle, New York prepares to greet its favorite meal. It is called brunch, and it is weird. . . . New Yorkers notoriously chafe at lines and delays, but come the weekend, they meekly tolerate a wait of 30 minutes for a crack at oysters on the half shell, baby spinach omelets and Irish steel-cut oatmeal. . . . What might Beringer have made of the "Sunday Strollers' Brunch" served at the Fifth Avenue Hotel in the 1940's, with its sauerkraut juice, its clam cocktails, its chicken liver omelet in Madeira, its calf's liver with hash browns, its Scotch woodcock? Or House & Garden's brunch recipe, offered in 1952, for rice almond pancakes served with herbed shad roe? "A delicate hash, light fish balls, and liver and bacon are all appropriate," one women's magazine wrote in the 1920's. New York is a tough town. No wonder its citizens wake up on Saturday and Sunday desperate for a little coddling, and ready for a spiritual return to the wholesome, abundant meals that good folks out in the heartland are eating. They want lemon ricotta pancakes, a lobster and arugula omelet, and a nice cold pitcher of tequila punch. What's so odd about that?[3]

Guy Beringer, whom Grimes names as the inventor of the word *brunch*, would hopefully be pleased with the plethora of simple and lavish brunch options that have emerged in a multitude of settings including hotels, restaurants, and museums. Brunch menus as exotic or familiar, as well as settings as commonplace or elaborate only continue to diversify. Brunching out historically began in hotels, then moved to restaurants, jazz clubs, churches, and most recently to museums.

BRUNCH HOTELS

In the early twentieth century, many restaurants were closed on Sundays, so eating brunch away from home really began in hotels and had its roots in the practice of serving breakfast to patrons of early boarding houses. Some of the earliest hotels to have had a brunch menu were in New York City—the Waldorf Astoria, the Fifth Avenue Hotel and the Plaza Hotel. In 1941, the Fifth Avenue Hotel advertised one of the earliest brunch menus, the "Sunday Strollers' Brunch,"[4] and by the 1940s, the Waldorf had a brunch menu that eventually would feature the infamous eggs Benedict, believed to have been ordered by Lemuel Benedict in 1942. According to one restaurant reviewer:

> The Waldorf Astoria has been serving a lavish Sunday brunch at its Peacock Alley Restaurant to its discerning guests for 40 years and remains the only NYC hotel to offer such an elaborate affair week after week. . . . The most popular dishes remain the classics: Eggs Benedict, which are made to order on house-made English muffins, Beef Wellington, carved by one of the friendly chefs on hand, and chilled North Atlantic lobster and oysters. The pastry chefs' display is always a big hit as well. Peacock Alley has been the place to be seen in Manhattan for many decades and Sunday Brunch extends the restaurant into the lobby and around the historic clock.[5]

The Waldorf Astoria continues to serve a highly regarded brunch to this day. Joshua Estrin of the *Huffington Post* recently reviewed the brunch: "Honored as an official New York City Landmark in 1993, recent renovations have reinvigorated the property, bringing it back to its original splendor." The Sunday brunch menu includes a raw bar with caviar, oysters, shrimp and crabs, smoked fish and meat carving stations, and newly added, and made in house "honey butter." The bees are actually living on top of the hotel as part of a New York City's green initiative.[6]

In 1969, the Biltmore on Madison Avenue in New York advertised a champagne brunch from 1 to 3 PM. By the 1970s, hotel brunches had increased in popularity but were sometimes seen with suspicion. In 1979, Florence Fabricant critically reviewed the United Nations Plaza Hotel's Ambassador Grill: "The big, all you can eat hotel buffet should also be ideal for families and they sound better than they are. As one hotel insider told us, the buffet is often a way of using up the week's leftovers from the banquet department. Even the most talked about buffet—in the U.N. Plaza Hotel's Ambassador Grill—presents dishes that look weary and warmed-over. The beef is shoulder, the salads dull, and the cherry-topped desserts could be twins of Sara Lee's."[7]

Hotels in California like the Beverly Wilshire and Alta Mira in Sausalito had started serving brunch by the mid-1960s. Santa Ynez in Los Angeles was serving baked filet of mahimahi for brunch.[8] Historic St. Petersburg, Florida, hotels such as the Vinoy Renaissance have been serving traditional upscale brunches since the 1970s. "Eggs in a Jar," also known as grits served with poached eggs and rock shrimp, helped make Marchand's at the Vinoy a brunch institution.

By the 1980s, brunch in hotels had become standard from Holiday Inns to the Four Seasons Dubai, the Intercontinental Chicago, or the Ritz Carlton Orlando. Despite the increase in offerings, middle-of-the-road brunch buffets in hotels became commonplace, and restaurant insiders continued to be critical of them.

BRUNCH RESTAURANTS

Who served the first brunch in a restaurant remains hazy. The first restaurant meals that might be considered brunches often weren't called brunch at all, but mid-morning or early afternoon meals or hybrids of second breakfasts or tea lunches. Many believe that America's first restaurant, Delmonico's in New York City, served the first versions of brunch, and by 1963, brunch was on its official menu.[9] Delmonico's chef Charles Ranhofer is also generally credited with inventing eggs Benedict, and this recipe appears in *The Epicurean* (1894).[10] Gael Greene was critical of brunch at Delmonico's by the 1970s when she wrote, "A sampler of hors d'oeuvre crammed onto a tiny saucer: the pate dull-tasting

Brunch at the Wolsely (*Courtesy of Travis Vande Berg*)

and dangerously grey . . . the rabbit terrine sharply gamy, with an odd fibrous texture . . . over poached salmon . . . rubbery aspic . . . sauce verte tasting like Miracle Whip tinted green."[11]

Along with Delmonico's, other New York City restaurants define the early history of restaurant brunches. By 1950, Tavern on the Green had an established brunch menu served from noon to 3 PM. Their 1971 Constitution brunch buffet included assorted egg and bread entrees, smoked fish, and bagels. The Rainbow Room, also in New York City, had its heyday in the 1930s as an elite supper club and had become infamous for its "Bloody Mary soup" by the 1960s. Promenade brunch in the Rainbow Room included menu items such as poached eggs with smoked salmon and caviar and challah bread French toast. By 1965, the Rainbow Room also advertised a Saturday brunch. Gaynor Maddox summarized the Rainbow Room's Saturday and Sunday brunch menus:

> The shorter the work week becomes, the more time for the leisurely brunch. It used to be a popular way to entertain late Sunday morning. But now, with so many people home on Saturday, hostesses attuned to the times are asking friends to Saturday brunch too. . . . Before planning your brunch, glance at the Rainbow Room menu: many kinds of fruit, then appetizers including smoked Brook Trout, Pate of Shrimp, chicken liver mousse, galantine of chicken. There are five soups including the amazing bloody mary. Next—six kinds of omelets, from sweetbreads to truffle sauce to curried crabmeat with chutney. Among other items in the main course are Grilled ham steak with glazed plum tarragon, calves liver and prosciutto, filet mignon in red wine with marrow and chives, and of course Eggs Benedict.[12]

Dessert options included tiny babas in flaming rum with ice cream to strawberry coupe or Swiss pastries.[13] Gael Greene also highlighted the Rainbow Room as one the most fabulous brunches in Manhattan in the 1970s:

Weird cravings for period vulgarity come and go, but when the thirties mood seizes, there is the Rainbow Room . . . as close to heaven as brunch can be . . . sixty-five flights up at 30 Rockefeller Plaza. The menu has some wild and promising flights of fancy, properly kinky for a $6.50 brunch; strawberry soup, pineapple with kirsch cream, curried herring in cream, an omelet with frogs' legs in truffle sauce. And the vol-au-vent of sweetbreads took the hotly contested first prize at an industry-sponsored Brunch fest. . . . Unwarmed bread, salted butter, bitterly over curried soup, blandly under curried crab-meat omelet. A curiously boring avocado Espanola. Cloyingly sweet kirsch cream killing the ripe tartness of fresh pineapple. Consommé served with a spill. The strawberry soup had an unpleasant taint of artificial flavor. At the peak of grumpiness, desserts arrived: an excellent buche au chocolat, ethereal vacherin glace, and dazzling Swiss pastry with a marzipan, chocolate-dipped goody that was quite memorable. Too bad man cannot live on marzipan alone.[14]

The Rainbow Room closed its kitchen in 2009.[15]

By 1966, Charley O's in Manhattan also served brunch. Greene reviewed Charley O's brunch in the 1970s:

The service is professional, pleasant, and unpressured. The coffee is excellent and Irish Milk Punch, $1.50, an inspired potion to cure any Sunday. . . . For the price of an entrée: melon and ground ginger, or grapefruit, or hot clam broth, or porridge with honey and cream; a great round loaf of crusty sesame-seed bread, slice it yourself; barmbrack—a rich raisin-and-candied-fruit-studded cake—and coffee. The porridge tastes like growing up in Vermont. Chicken hash turned out to be merely creamed chunks of chicken in a crumb-topped cream sauce. The bacon, potato, and onion omelet ($3.95) might have been softer through the middle but the gentlemen who ordered it thought it as perfect.[16]

In the 1960s, brunch was catching on in restaurants outside of New York City as well. By 1966, brunch had become popular at

Trader Vic's in San Francisco. The Grill Room in Washington, D.C., has been hosting brunch since at least the 1970s.

Chicago has also had a vibrant brunch and breakfast scene since the 1950s. Lou Mitchell's, which opened in 1949, preceded the big brunch trend. It began as a coffee shop and eventually became a breakfast then a brunch institution. On weekends, customers often wait over an hour to dine in this small historic diner, receiving donut holes while they wait. While the restaurant boasts of "serving the world's best coffee," this is an alcohol-free diner.[17] Portland, Oregon, is where the Original Pancake House had its first location in 1953, but the Walker brothers opened the Chicago area's first Original Pancake House in the northern Chicago suburb of Wilmette in 1960.[18] IHOP had already opened in 1958.[19]

By the 1970s, brunch had truly arrived in Chicago's restaurant scene. The infamous Roger Park's Heartland Café has been serving up progressive politics and crunchy fare since 1976. The Blind Faith Café opened in Evanston in 1979 and offers vegetarian and vegan versions of popular Mexican brunch fare such as Aztec hash and seitan chorizo omelet. Down the street, also in Evanston, the Lucky Platter has been serving its brand of hippy and eclectic brunch since1982.[20] Ann Sather's became a Chicago breakfast and brunch institution by the 1970s, famous for their Swedish pancakes with lingonberries and enormous cinnamon buns. The Chicago Diner opened its doors in 1983, and Clarke's has several restaurants throughout the Chicago area.

In the last few decades, Chicago has also become the home of many trendy bruncheries. Wishbone's Southern fare has made it a brunch hotspot. Bongo Room signaled the beginning of the gentrification in Chicago's Wicker Park neighborhood and has offered up trendy breakfast burritos, vegan cinnamon rolls, and tofu Benedict since the 1990s. Big Jones opened in 2008 and serves Southern low-country cooking for brunch in the Andersonville,

Chicago, neighborhood. Its chef uses historic recipes including popovers from a historic Edna Lewis recipe, Sally Lunn (an old English breakfast good), and awendaw (an ancient spoon bread/ cornmeal breakfast recipe). [21]

Since the 1980s, brunch in restaurants has begun to reflect the diversity in the American culinary landscape by going global, organic, and green. Dim sum had always been a brunch option in California and New York City, but during this decade, we saw the proliferation of ethnic brunches particularly including the spread of Mexican and Southern brunches. In the 1990s, brunch out began to slowly reflect the green movement and we saw the popularity of simpler and trendy brunches also including more vegetarian options. In the last decade, we continue to see both a shift to farm-to-table brunches as well as the romanticization of rural, Midwestern, and Southern brunches, with the proliferation of brunch spots such as the Farm on Adderly, Friend of a Farmer, Picket Fence, Buttermilk, and Tipsy Parson in New York City. Sarabeth's, from *Gossip Girl* fame, has been a New York City institution since 1981 (and now has multiple locations).These hip brunch spots reinvent traditional, often Midwestern and Southern, brunch classics. Fried chicken and waffles, and biscuits and gravy show up at trendy brunch spots, but we also see some of these trends reflected in restaurant chains. Outside of New York City, only a few hours away, Hattie's in Saratoga serves a Sunday brunch that showcases fried chicken and waffles. Not too far from Saratoga, in Ithaca, Northstar gastropub and restaurant dishes up locavore brunch dishes every Sunday, including their famous French toast with local berries and tofu scramble.

In other parts of the United States, brunch classics continue to also be served in popular restaurant chains such as International House of Pancakes, Waffle House, Denny's, and the Original Pancake House. Other restaurant chains such as Cheesecake Fac-

Biscuits and gravy (Photo by Heather Bohn-Tallman; http://hbtphoto. pass.us/hatties-brunch-1/i-9mByt77949648; from Heather Bohm-Tallman photography, http://hbtphoto.blogspot.com/)

tory, Bonefish Grill, Mimi's Café, and First Watch serve special brunch items on weekends.

Many of the more mid-level chains that now serve brunch started in Florida, which has recently adapted brunch to its own "Floribean" cuisine. The Rusty Pelican and Oystercatcher's on Tampa/St. Petersburg's Causeway offer seafood brunch buffets complete with crab legs and omelet stations. You can often see them pulling your seafood out of the water while you are dining. Lump crab quiche and lobster omelet also reflect St. Petersburg's traditional culinary history and local oceanside cuisine. In recent restaurant reviews, the evolving brunch scene in Tampa was best summed up by Jeff Houck as "Tampa Bay chefs get creative."[22] More recently, innovative weekend brunches that showcase Florida's regional and local ingredients can be enjoyed at The Refinery, Boca, Piquante, and Oxford Exchange in Tampa Bay. The Refinery, one of a few James Beard nominees in Tampa, has one of the most diverse brunch menus, including eggs with fried chicken livers and collard greens as well as huevos rancheros served with frijoles charros and cheese grits. At Boca, you can enjoy Cuban eggs Benedict, and Ella's Americana Art Café does soul food Sundays when they serve fried chicken and waffles all day.[23]

Brunching out has always been more prevalent among the middle class, but in the last few decades, where you brunch is also indicative of personal food politics as well as cyclical trends. Eating organic, local, vegetarian, or gluten free also continues to shape options for brunching out.

BRUNCH AT CHURCH

In many ways, it's a surprise that more places of worship don't serve brunch after services, since brunching out after church has been a popular tradition with American families for years. However, there are mosques, temples, and churches that do serve brunch after services. Often these special meals are served around important religious holidays, but some religious institutions have incorporated brunches into their weekly services. For example, Cavalry Church outside of Chicago offers a full-service brunch in a restaurant on its premises,[24] and Asbury United

Methodist Church in Texas hosts a potluck brunch once a month.[25]

In Berkeley, a Thai brunch at a Buddhist temple became so popular with Thai families and local foodies that it created a controversy:

> The food service expanded gradually from a small gathering of Thai families to a must-eat event, as word spread among local residents and college students. As brunch has grown, so has the temple. . . . Opponents in the neighborhood have argued that the temple doesn't need all of the money generated by weekly brunch to support its activities. . . . In an effort to appease neighbors, the temple agreed during mediation sessions to cut the hours for brunch service in half.[26]

Brunch after Jewish services can be found at some synagogues and temples, often featuring lox and bagels and cream cheese.[27] After Friday prayer, many American Islamic centers in urban areas serve brunch featuring Arab and Pakistani specialties. The Scientology center in California also has a brunch service at their restaurant.

These weekend brunches offer social networking opportunities for religious minorities in urban centers. Sharing a meal together after worship is a tradition shared by many religious groups.

BRUNCH AT MUSEUMS

Since the 1970s, established museums have also been serving brunch. Brunch at a museum usually involves fine dining in one of the most aesthetically pleasing settings. The Metropolitan Museum of Art's Fountain Restaurant serves weekend brunches with traditional fare and a full bar.[28] They even take reservations. Untitled, the farm-to-table restaurant at New York City's Whitney Museum, also serves weekend brunches. One reviewer remarked:

It is the simplicity of the dishes that allow you to taste the excellent quality of the food and great flavors. The farm-to-table restaurant serves the freshest ingredients and edibles from local farms and businesses. . . . The poached egg with cheese grits and chard was simple perfection. And, we couldn't help but eye a few times over the "From the Griddle" portion of the menu [which] included huckleberry pancakes and banana & hazelnut stuffed French toast. . . . It may be easy to forget about a brunch spot in the basement of a museum, but . . . the brunch fare here at Untitled will definitely stay on your mind.[29]

In Chicago, the Museum of Contemporary Art serves a special brunch on Sundays by Wolfgang Puck, and the Art Institute in Chicago serves a Sunday brunch with an Italian flair. Museums in major metropolitan centers serve substantial meals, and many of them now serve Sunday brunch.

Outside of the United States, there are many museums where you can have a lovely breakfast or brunch. In 2013, the restaurant at the Acropolis Museum in Athens began to serve a traditional breakfast and brunch. "It is worth a visit to try the galatopita (milk pie), tiganites (Greek pancakes) with tahini and petimezi (grape molasses), trahana (pellet-shaped pasta made with milk) with feta cheese and the omelet with the famous gravicra cheese from the island of Naxos, as well as the siglino (smoked pork) from Mani."[30]

JAZZ AND GOSPEL BRUNCHES

Jazz and gospel brunches follow two intersecting trajectories. Jazz brunches seemed to have originated in New Orleans, and gospel brunches are often traced to Harlem in New York. Chicago seems to be at the center point where both jazz and gospel brunches flourished by the 1980s. New Orleans boasts the "world's largest jazz brunch" in their annual French Quarter festival.[31]

There is some controversy as to the origins of the jazz brunch. Mr. Kelly's on Rush Street in Chicago debuted a jazz brunch in 1971, which the *Chicago Defender* claims was the origin of the jazz brunch.[32] For $2.95, patrons could enjoy music and a menu that included, "beef hash served with poached egg and tomato sauce, scrambled eggs with bacon or sausage and potatoes, and honey dipped fried chicken served with potatoes, gravy and peas."[33] However, the *New York Times* traces the origins of the jazz brunch to the Commander's Palace: "Ella Brennan, Commander's co-owner, recalls hiring jazz musicians in 1973 to enliven slow Sundays at the restaurant, some years after she and her family made breakfast at Brennan's into a celebrity event in the family's French Quarter restaurant."[34]

Regardless of this controversy, the jazz brunch itself is often synonymous with New Orleans and the innovation, according to Mark Huntsman, is "perhaps the most important incarnation of brunch, culturally speaking." He continues, "Louisianans have left a local stamp on a concept (brunch) currently put into practice all throughout the nation and the world."[35] Huntsman breaks down the rules of the jazz brunch to the following: (1) the jazz brunch is held on Sunday, (2) it should be relaxing, (3) the music is in the background and the emphasis is on food and socializing. Restaurant-specific egg dishes are particularly important:

> While not all restaurants have created their own signature egg dish for the jazz brunch, many of the oldest, choicest, and most famous places such as Arnaud's, Commander's Palace, and Brennan's, have done so. . . . Certainly, tourists have demands as well that may be different from those of locals . . . but locals are responsible for incorporating existing gastronomic traditions into the tradition of jazz brunch. For example, grits and grillades are often thought of as one of the quintessential Creole breakfast foods (as well as a staple of Mardi Gras), a cultu-

ral tradition so strong that it overrides other sentiments such as class division: this very humble dish, once eaten primarily by the lowest classes, is even part of the jazz brunch menu at Antoine's, available with premium veal cutlets and extra-buttery grits for $19.75. Antoine's has bought into this tradition because its patrons have requested it—the same reason that Muriel's began serving jazz brunch in the first place.[36]

Variations of jazz brunches spread outside of Louisiana by the 1970s.

Like the jazz brunch, the gospel brunch is also a hybrid of food and music but adds a touch of spirituality. Like the jazz brunch, there is some controversy as to its origins. However, Leslie Gourse in the *Los Angeles Times* traces gospel brunches to Lola's in Manhattan in 1985:

> The gospel brunch was born 13 years ago when a midtown Manhattan restaurant, Lola's, hired singers from Pentecostal and Baptist churches in Queens and Brooklyn to entertain at Sunday brunch. It was such a hit that Lola's had to expand the brunch to accommodate three seatings. A few years later, the gospel brunch surfaced in Harlem, where it has become an entertaining postscript to serious Sunday morning churchgoing. While people of all races and faiths enjoy gospel brunches, European and Japanese fans of American music, especially jazz, seem to predominate among the tourists. For New Yorkers, the music definitely provides a respite from the intense pace of life on weekdays. The catchy hymns and spirituals give people a chance to let their hair down and dance, pray, cry and laugh all at the same time. Word of mouth helped spread Lola's reputation. "Be sure to go to Lola's on Sundays," tourists returning home have told their friends setting out for vacations in New York.[37]

One place of particular importance to the history of both jazz and gospel brunches is Sylvia's in Harlem, where nostalgia for the Harlem Renaissance and the jazz age merged great food with music. Sylvia's began hosting jazz brunches on Saturdays and gospel brunches on Sundays, both featuring Southern soul food dishes. One reviewer summarized the menu at Sylvia's as including "everything from Southern fried chicken, grits, and cornmeal fried whitening for breakfast to stewed turkey wings and Southern style chitterlings for a daily special, and Harlem styled waffles and golden fried ribs for an entrée. (I would suggest the baked macaroni & cheese and candied yams for your side orders.) Oh, and don't forget your strawberry bread pudding with bourbon sauce for dessert."[38]

Both jazz and gospel brunches have spread beyond their original restaurants and cities and can now be found all over the United States and throughout the world.

BRUNCH OUTSIDE THE WEST

Wherever a middle class with disposable income emerges, brunch seems to surely follow. Some of the most lavish displays of brunch and conspicuous consumption are outside the Western world. Eating brunch in hotels or restaurants is not only an American tradition. You can go to any major metropolitan city from London to Paris to Amsterdam and find a brunch option on the weekend, and brunch in some of the less predictable urban destinations like Tokyo, Mumbai, Dubai, and Istanbul are some of the most extravagant of all. Both Mumbai and Dubai have developed quite the reputation for brunching as an indication of wealth.

In 1957, the Imperial Hotel in Tokyo opened the first Viking buffet,[39] and today many luxury hotels in Tokyo have this as a lunch or weekend brunch option.[40] The Viking buffet was adapted from the Swedish smorgasbord tradition and is a hotel buffet usually served on weekends that includes Japanese and Western brunch and lunch options including sushi, omelets, and bacon.

Brunch in India has also come to represent wealth, and some of the country's most impressive and luxurious brunches are in restaurants and hotels that blend culinary traditions of West and East. In India, we can also see evidence of a fusion of sorts at Sunday brunch on Easter, and traditional brunch dishes such as eggs and pancakes and eggs Benedict can also be found on menus in Delhi.[41] Mumbai's over-the-top brunch scene is only second to Dubai's.

Dubai's dining scene has been catering to tourists, celebrities, and elite Arab society for several decades, and brunch out in Dubai is quite the decadent experience.[42] Brunch in Dubai is on Friday rather than Sunday, as it follows the Islamic calendar and weekends begin on Thursday nights. A BBC report on brunch in Dubai states that Dubai's version of brunch "has always tended towards an orgy of excess—eating and drinking so much that the atmosphere feels more akin to a late Saturday night than a Friday afternoon."[43] Similarly, top hotels in Cairo, Beirut, and Jerusalem also serve lavish brunches on the weekends.

Just outside of the Middle East, we can go to Istanbul and Athens for a sampling of East-meets-West brunches. In Athens, hotels since the 1960s have offered weekend breakfast buffets. Sofia's Valaoritou Café in Athens is known for its truffles, artichokes, and spinach feta tarts.[44] The Athens Hilton also provides a touristy Sunday hotel brunch at their restaurant, Byzantino, which offers the likes of French toast and croissants next to platters of mousaka. The Seasons Restaurant's Sunday brunch, chosen by leading gourmets and foodies as "Istanbul's Best Brunch," can be savored every Sunday from 11:30 AM onward, and the food includes sushi rolls, French pastries, and barbecued lamb.

Closer to home, Americans in particular often brunch out in hotels when vacationing in Puerto Rico and other parts of the Caribbean. All-inclusive resorts have been offering brunches since the 1950s. In San Juan, all you can eat brunch buffets in-

clude traditional guava pastries, roasted pork and beans, and seafood options.[45] Hotels in Mexico City were quick to adapt huevos
rancheros (rancher's eggs, which are tortillas and eggs, served
with chili sauce and often beans), huevos albaniles (bricklayers
eggs), and huevos motulenos (eggs from Motul that are eggs in
tortillas with ham and peas). Many of these Mexican egg dishes
have made it onto brunch menus in the American Southwest.[46]
More recently, celebrity chefs like Rick Bayless have further popularized Mexican breakfast and brunch dishes through cookbooks
and popular restaurants.

No matter where one travels, urbanized centers offer a diverse
array of brunch options in hotels and restaurants. Brunch has
become an important part of restaurant culture, especially in the
United States. Americans in New York, Chicago, and even Portland will often wait in line for more than ninety minutes for the
hippest brunch, and television, as well as social media, has played
a role in keeping brunch on trend.

5

BRUNCH IN POPULAR CULTURE

When does a trend become a part of popular culture? When it's featured in the *New York Times* or on Twitter? In 2012's *Portlandia* episode "Brunch Village," Peter and Nance line up behind hundreds along several streets to eat at the newest hipster brunch spot, "Fisherman's Porch." Brunch in television and film reflects how brunch is shaped by gender, class, and changing social norms. Brunch is also an important meal in contemporary films, especially wedding-themed films such as *The Hangover Part II*. Brunch has also become a popular theme in fiction, especially "chick lit." This chapter explores brunch in popular culture.

Brunch has been featured in many television shows and movies, especially once the brunch meal had become part of American culture and seeped into the middle class after the 1960s. One of the earliest references to brunch in television was in 1962 on *The Dick Van Dyke Show* when Rob Petrie (Dick Van Dyke) complements his wife, Laura (Mary Tyler Moore), on her brunch outfit.

Brunch signaled comfort and home for the characters of the 1972–1983 sitcom *M*A*S*H*, which centered on a mobile army surgical hospital during the Korean War. In the 1982 episode "A Holy Mess," a poultry farmer donates a day's worth of eggs to their unit. They haven't had fresh eggs in so long the idea of a brunch with eggs makes them all very excited to the point where they start giving individual orders to the cook on how to prepare their eggs. A few of them even sneak into the kitchen to prepare omelets and soft-boiled eggs because the cook refuses to serve anything but scrambled. In the end, everyone is just happy to have fresh eggs, and the brunch turns into a picnic.

The recent film *It's a Disaster*, starring David Cross and Julia Stiles, takes place during one couple's long brunch at a home in Los Angeles as the world is coming to an end. And of course, there are television shows that are themed around brunch time on weekends. *Brunch with Bobby* is on Saturdays at 1 PM on the Cooking Channel. The first season aired in 2010. Tim Lovejoy and Simon Rimmer host *Sunday Brunch* on BBC as a weekend morning talk show, which features celebrity guests, cooking demonstrations, and conversation. Of greater interest, however, are the larger themes conveyed by the use of brunch.

BRUNCH IN TELEVISION AND FILMS

One way that brunch has been humorously discussed in popular culture has to do with the nature of the meal itself and its combination of breakfast and lunch foods and traditions. In the 1990s, the iconic television comedies *The Simpsons* and *Seinfeld* both mention brunch in this way. In the 1990 episode of *The Simpsons* "Life on the Fast Lane," Jacques Cousteau, a bowling instructor at Barney's Bowlarama, asks Marge to brunch, explaining that brunch is "not quite breakfast, it's not quite lunch, but it comes with a slice of cantaloupe at the end. You don't get completely what you would at breakfast, but you get a good meal."[1] Similarly, in the 1996 *Seinfeld* episode "The Invitations," Jerry is dating a woman who appears to be a female version of himself (played by Janeane Garafalo). Over a bowl of cereal, Garafalo's character asks Jerry, "Hey! So what's the deal with brunch? I mean that if it's a combination of breakfast and lunch, how comes there's no lupper or no linner?"[2]

The permissive indulgence of brunch has also been highlighted on television shows, like an episode of popular CBS sitcom *The Big Bang Theory*. Penny, Bernadette, and Amy go to brunch and have a conversation about the meal. Penny declares, "Ah, [brunch is] the best! You have booze with breakfast on a Tuesday you got a problem. You do it on a weekend you got brunch." Amy (Sheldon's girlfriend on the show) adds, "Sheldon doesn't believe in brunch. He can't stand being at a table where one person's having an omelet and another person's having a sandwich."[3] Penny is consistently the outsider of the characters on this show, and she is also the one more comfortable drinking during the day, and appreciates the concept that alcoholic drinks are welcome on a weekend brunch. Sheldon doesn't believe in brunch because Sheldon likes clear distinctions and boundaries for life and his meals. This is indicative of both Sheldon's personality and what brunch means to these characters (and more generally in popular culture). Sheldon's character always wants order and tends to follow rules meticulously. But brunch suggests disorder and chaos as almost any kind of food can be eaten at brunch.

The role of alcohol in brunch is also humorously portrayed on an episode of *Arrested Development*, a Fox and now Netflix sitcom centered on the wealthy and self-centered Bluth family. Michael (Jason Bateman) has brunch at Skip Church's Bistro when getting to know Sally Sitwell, but while waiting for a table Sally says, "I still can't believe we got in. This place is usually so packed on Sundays." The narrator (Ron Howard) explains, "In addition to brunch, the restaurant was known for an item on the menu called the 'Skip's Scramble,' an omelet that contained everything on the menu. Do not order the Skip's Scramble."[4] While Michael and Sally are brunching at one table, Michael's son, George Michael, and his niece, Maeby, are sharing what they think are brunch cocktails at another table. Maeby tells George Michael, "You know, George Michael, you worry too much. It's Sunday. You're allowed to have a couple of hours off. You don't see me nervous about being on my third Virgin Mary." George Michael responds, "Why would you be nervous? There's no alcohol in a Virgin Mary." Distraught, Maeby orders again: "There isn't? This is unbelievable. Can I get a virgin Piña Colada when you get a chance? Now we'll get things started." Brunch gives the underage Maeby permission to drink during the day (though she only ends up drinking virgin cocktails), but brunch is commonplace among the upper-crust Bluth family, who overindulge in daytime drinking pretty regularly.

This sort of conspicuous consumption and bad behavior also shows up on reality television. *The Real Housewives of New York* has an episode titled "Boozy Brunch" and features the housewives doing brunch in downtown Manhattan. Jimmy Fallon's late-night talk show later parodied this sort of brunch behavior with Denise "the queen of late night" (played by Fallon) hosting a Real Housewives Brunch.

CLASS STATUS AND BRUNCH

Brunch as a sign of class status has been one of the most prevalent ways that brunch has been portrayed in popular culture. The classic sitcom *All in the Family* regularly depicted conflicts over societal norms and events, "traditional" and "liberal" values, and class—particularly working class—experiences. The 1971 pilot episode of the show features an anniversary brunch for Archie and Edith. Archie and Edith's daughter Gloria and her partner Michael plan an anniversary brunch for Archie and Edith while they are at church. While they are getting brunch ready, Gloria says to Michael, "It's different isn't it, an anniversary brunch?"

who responds, "Yeah, well I think your mother will love it, but your father doesn't care about anniversaries." When Edith and Archie arrive home early from church to the surprise brunch, Edith is happy and comments, "The table is all set . . . they have made us a brunch." Archie, however, isn't interested in brunch, which he sees as some new bourgeoisie ritual: "Brunch, it figures. She's reading *Cosmopolitan*." Gloria escorts her parents through the house: "Well here we are, we have the orange juice in here and we go in there for brunch." Edith responds, "My, my how fancy." Later during the brunch, Gloria chides Archie not to put ketchup on eggs: "Ketchup on eggs, Daddy? Really?" Archie disparagingly responds, "Ketchup on eggs is what we've been eating since before you were born. Don't let it concern you." As is consistent with the entire series, Gloria has aspirations to be more educated, sophisticated, and middle class while Archie is comfortable with who he is—white and working class—and brunch in this episode clearly symbolizes this tension. The brunch ends up in chaos with Michael and Archie arguing about poverty, unemployment, religion, and race.

Brunch also signals class or what's perceived as respectable and classy in the popular sitcom *Three's Company*, which featured "The Brunch" as an episode in 1982. This episode is focused around Jack trying to make his "Jack's Bistro" successful, but he hasn't been able to secure a liquor license. Jack's primary investor, Mr. Angelino, tells him that a conservative minister is keeping his restaurant from getting a liquor license because it was once a place that prostitutes spent time. Jack and Mr. Angelino believe that serving a champagne brunch will help convince the minister that Jack's restaurant is a respectable place. Here, obviously, brunch is perceived as classy and champagne symbolizes "upscale." Jack serves eggs Benedict a la Jacque, and his champagne brunch is a success because he manages to fill the bistro with respectable and conservatively dressed guests including Janet and Terry in modest dresses, Larry with a date, and an older woman who happens to be a church donor. The minister shows up for the brunch and isn't sure if a bistro serving champagne and promoting daytime drinking is the kind of establishment he wants to support. Ultimately, the church donor insists that Jack's Bistro is a classy place that made her feel welcome, which secures the minister's support for Jack's liquor license.

The 1991 comedy *LA Story*, starring Steve Martin, also featured a brunch scene connected to class. Steve Martin's character and his girlfriend meet friends for brunch at the Ambassador Hotel in Los Angeles. There is a harp playing in the background, and the camera pans to the carefully piled pastries next to one of the carving stations. The group's ordering is a perfect example of class pretension at brunch when one friend orders, "I'll have a double decaf cappuccino," and another says, "I'll have a half double decaffeinated half-caf, with a twist of lemon."[5]

Two successful NBC sitcoms also portrayed brunch as a sign of class and respectability. *Frasier* was often infused with class-based humor and frequently pokes fun at Frasier Crane's class aspirations and pretensions, and the juxtaposition of Frasier and his brother Niles with their blue-collar father, Martin. Frasier and Niles's knowledge and consumption of fine food and wine is an ever-present theme on this show; their display of culinary capital is one way that they mark their cultured and upper-crust sensibilities.[6] Brunch is prominently featured in the show's 2000 episode "The Whine Club." In this episode, Niles uses brunch in order to introduce his family to his new girlfriend, Mel, but the meal also becomes a platform for Frasier to antagonize Niles about their contentious leadership roles in their wine club. Roz clearly dislikes Mel and bluntly asks, "When you invited me, did you say 'brunch for Mel' or 'brunch from Hell'?" In the end, Mel enjoys the brunch, calling it "such a civilized way to spend an afternoon." Brunch, again, is a classy and civilized way to socialize.[7]

The NBC sitcom, *Will and Grace*, centered on Grace, a heterosexual interior designer, and her gay roommate, Will, a successful attorney, living in Manhattan. Brunch at the upscale Manhattan Plaza Hotel is featured in the 2002 episode "The Needle and the Omelet's Done." Grace clearly has aspirational upper-class dreams, and is overly excited to brunch at the Plaza with Leo (Harry Connick Jr.). Grace prepares by reviewing the brunch layout the week before and explains to Leo her strategy for enjoying the Plaza's buffet: "Okay, the key to a successful brunch strategy is knowing how to work the buffet. See, they put all the cheap stuff, like scones and muffins, in front. I mean, how many of those can you have? Eight? Ten? That's like four bucks. Meanwhile, the smoked fishes and other pricey items are around the corner." Grace is also more than eager to enjoy the relaxed social norms associated with drinking during the day when brunching, and she remarks, "Please, sit. We just ordered mimosas, which I believe is French for 'I don't wanna wait till noon to get hammered.'" Grace's over-the-top character is determined to take advantage of the Plaza's all-you-can-eat decadent brunch buffet, and she does![8]

Perhaps no show has made the class connotations of brunch as clear as the popular American teen drama *Gossip Girl*, which aired on The CW from 2007 to 2012. The show focused on the everyday lives of privileged teenagers living on the Upper East Side of Manhattan and featured an emphasis on luxury and leisure. The characters on the show often dine at exclusive restaurants in Manhattan, and the second episode of the series, "The Wild Brunch," features a brunch thrown at the Palace by Chuck Bass and his father. The episode opens with the Gossip Girl narrating: "Upper East Siders don't do lazy Sundays. Lazy Sundays are for po' people. That's why they're po' in the first place, because they are so darn lazy. Denizens of the Upper East Side do brunch on Sundays, and on this particular day, Chuck Bass's silver fox father is hosting a brunch for his foundation at the Palace.

Everybody who's anybody is invited, which means, of course, that the Humphreys are decidedly not."[9]

GENDER ROLES AND BRUNCH

In addition to being portrayed as decadent, classy, and without rules, brunch has also been depicted as a gendered meal in television and movies. Before *Gossip Girl*, *Sex and the City* symbolized unattainable Manhattan and regularly featured the four women lunching or brunching at popular brunch spots such as Pastis and Balthazar's. In one episode of the show, Carrie (Sarah Jessica Parker) explains the significance of brunch, especially to New Yorkers and, more specifically, to female New Yorkers: "There are very few things this New Yorker loves as much as Sunday brunch. You can sleep until noon and still get eggs anywhere in the city, alcohol is often included with the meal, and Sunday is the one day a week you get the single woman's sports pages: the *New York Times* wedding section."[10] *Sex and the City* served to popularize the idea of the women's brunch or "girls' brunch." On the NBC sitcom *30 Rock*, Liz Lemon (Tina Fey) tells her boss Jack that she's ready for one of those "*Sex and the City* girls' brunches,"[11] so she can talk about her sex life. These "girls' brunches" are also at the heart of several episodes in the *Real Housewives* series as discussed above.

The gendered nature of brunch is also humorously addressed on *How I Met Your Mother*, the popular CBS sitcom centered around the lives of five young professionals living in New York. Marshall is single and starts spending time with his recently single friend Brad. They go to dinner, the theater, and even brunch. Marshall's friends make it clear that brunch is for couples or women, leading Marshall to ask Ted, "Why can't two guys who are friends go to brunch?" Ted replies, "Because brunch is kind of . . ." and Robin quickly interjects, "Girlie." Ted and Robin declaring that brunch is girlie further exasperates Marshall, and he responds, "Girlie? Breakfast isn't girlie; lunch isn't girlie, what makes brunch girlie?" To which Ted says, "I don't know . . . nothing girlie about a horse, nothing girlie about a horn . . . but put them together and you get a unicorn." When Marshall does go to brunch with male friend Brad, he declares, "God, I love brunch." Brad agrees and says, "I mean, why can't two single bros go out and rock brunch Sunday morning–style?" Later in the episode, Marshall starts putting all of what he thinks are the clues (including their brunch outing) together and concludes that Brad is gay and has a crush on him (neither is true).[12] Like in *Sex and the City* and *30 Rock*, brunch out is represented as a women's social ritual.

EVENT BRUNCHES

Brunch has also been used in popular culture to mark important events or holidays. The most frequent of these is the depiction of the wedding-associated brunch. This is the case in the 1975 episode of *The Mary Tyler Moore Show* called "Ted's Wedding." In this episode, a long-running joke on the show that Ted frequently proposes marriage to Georgette and then never follows through on the actual wedding is finally resolved. The episode begins with Mary hosting Georgette and Ted for brunch because she feels bad about never including him at work. During the brunch Ted says, "You look gorgeous, Georgette. I love you. Will you marry me?" Georgette responds, "So what do you say, buster, you still want to get married?" and Ted replies, "Yes, I do." Georgette finally called Ted's bluff, and Mary helps Georgette throw together a last-minute wedding following brunch.[13]

The 2001 film *My Best Friend's Wedding*, starring Julia Roberts and Cameron Diaz, features a pre-wedding brunch held at one of the character's parents' estate. The two film versions of *Sex and the City* also prominently featured wedding brunches. In the first film (2008's *Sex and the City*), Carrie and Big meet Samantha, Charlotte, Miranda, and their partners for a small surprise brunch following Carrie and Big's simple wedding with a justice of the peace. In *Sex and the City 2* Samantha invites all the girls to Abu Dubai over brunch.

In a combined highlighting of both gender roles and brunches associated with weddings, we have Stu in *The Hangover Part II* asking for a bachelor brunch in place of the traditional bachelor party. Stu explains to the other guys, "Yeah! It's my bachelor brunch. Go crazy. Get some chocolate chip pancakes, a lap dance from the waitress." His friend Phil responds, "Well, I refuse to eat fucking cantaloupe at a bachelor party!"[14] Of course, in expected *Hangover* tradition, the brunch does not go as planned, and the guys sabotage Stu's plans for a bachelor brunch, as they clearly don't think a brunch is an acceptable alternative to a bachelor party. Brunch parties are either for women as showers or for couples as part of the wedding weekend, but these dudes still don't brunch.

THE RISE OF THE HIPSTER BRUNCH

Brunch in both television and film has tended to symbolize gender, class, shifts in culture, overindulgence, and conspicuous consumption, and recently, there have been several parodies of these aspects of brunch. Television shows as *The Sarah Silverman Program* and *Portlandia* have provided satires of brunch as a liberal, middle-class, (and often-white) hipster trend.

In the third season episode of *The Sarah Silverman Program* "Night Mayor," Mayor Kadoody wants to outlaw both gay marriage and brunch, seeing them both as indicative of the spread of liberal values. However, ironically, Sarah Silverman proclaims, "Mayor Kadoody is gay and she was caught with eggs between the hours of 11 and 1 p.m." Silverman tries to explain that brunch is harmless and is just combining eggs and 11 o'clock.

The best parody of brunch is probably found in the 2012 "Brunch Village" episode of the IFC comedy show *Portlandia*. (The episode spawned a special hour-long version called "Brunch Special" as well.) The show famously satirizes of white, middle-class, hipster norms in Portland, Oregon, and this episode pokes fun at the lengths the residents will go to brunch at the newest, trendiest restaurant. Everyone in Portland wants to eat at the trendy Fisherman's Porch for brunch, including all of the show's recurring characters. There are customers lined up around the block, and people are camped out with tents and coolers. Some customers have a five-hour wait, and there are even two bouncers who keep the customers in line and penalize them if they cut the line. Two of the characters, Peter and Nance, are so exhausted by the time they are called for brunch that they have to be carried through on customers' shoulders. Meanwhile Carrie and Fred are supposed to meet the mayor for brunch in the same hip neighborhood and assume that the mayor must also want to eat at Fisherman's Porch since it's the hot new brunch spot. But the mayor (Kyle MacLachlan) arrives via kayak several hours late, all along wanting to have brunch at Ed Begley's tiny and very unpopular diner. "Brunch Village" is a social commentary on how in certain cities brunch culture has evolved into a "scene" among the creative class; the aspirational class of artists and young professionals; and, most recently, the hipsters who will go to any length to attain and consume the next hip culinary trend.

Overall, brunch in recent years signals both class and hipster norms. The creative class is quick to consume the next up-and-coming food trend, often as an indication of their culinary capital. Both their knowledge and consumption of food trends is a way for them to establish status, especially in hip and urban settings like Portland.

BRUNCH IN MUSIC

As brunching at home grew in popularity as a way to entertain friends and family on the weekend, it needed a soundtrack. Popular brunch compilations since the 1990s often featured classical music or smooth jazz. In 1995, *Let's Do Brunch* featured classical compositions by Haydn, Vivaldi, Mozart, Torelli, and Chopin, and 1996's *Brunch* featured compositions by Vivaldi, Handel, Telemann, Boccherini, and Bach. In 2004, two brunch compilations were released that featured classical music: *For Sunday Brunch* featured Bach, Telemann, Boccherini, Handel, and Grieg; and *Sunday Morning Brunch* featured Strauss, Tchaikovsky, Chopin, Mozart, and Beethoven. These brunch compilations featured classical music that became synonymous with the middle-class ritual of relaxing music and brunch in the morning. Jazz and gospel music has also become a common soundtrack for brunch.

Like the class and status theme seen in television and movie depictions of brunch, brunch in popular music often signifies the "the good life." This important theme signals both the spread of brunch's popularity but also brunch's coded class status. For example, on "Millionaire Blues," a song on Dire Straits' 1991 album *Every Street*, Mark Knopfler sings about a champagne brunch—a sure sign of class and success. This trend has been even more apparent in R&B, hip-hop, and rap music since the 1990s. In 1991, "What" on the A Tribe Called Quest album *The Low End Theory* references questioning those that don't like brunch. In 2001, Jay-Z released *The Blueprint* on which he raps about how he used to have lunch in his old neighborhood but now he should be having brunch at the Four Seasons on the song "Song Cry." On 2009's *Relapse*, Eminem raps about having red wine for brunch in "Bagpipes from Baghdad." In "Too Many Rappers" from the Beastie Boys' 2011 album, *Hot Sauce Committee Part Two*, MCA raps about preparing brunch for MCs at his house. In these and other songs, brunch seems to accompany the blinged-out life as well as "making it" as a theme in many of these songs.

Other themes arise in songs mentioning brunch, including brunch as related to weddings and love, and the gendered nature of brunching. In 1996, country singer Randy Travis sings about making brunch for his "baby" on the song "Would I," and Prince sings about brunch as part of a wedding event on 2001's "Wedding Feast." Barbara Streisand's 2002 album *The Broadway Album* featured Stephen Sondheim's song "The Ladies Who Lunch" from the musical *Company*. In the song, the titular ladies have too much time on their hands and are planning a brunch.

In 1980, Blondie's *Auto American* featured brunch in the song, "Faces." In 2010, Sarah Silverman released *Songs of the Sarah Silverman Program: From Our Rears to Your Ears!* on which appears "Meaning of Brunch."

BRUNCH FICTION

Brunch in fiction has probably made its biggest splash in women's fiction or "chick lit." Chick lit, catering to a women's audience, often focuses on themes of romance and female friendship.

Melissa Banks's 2000 novel, *The Girls' Guide to Hunting and Fishing*, has a brunch scene of simple lox and bagels before a family funeral.[15] In 2001's *No; Maybe Yes* by Pamela Hollins, Carol and Jenny develop a monthly tradition of going to brunch as they search for love and bonding, much like in *Sex and the City*.[16] In Jennifer Weiner's novel *Good in Bed*, the protagonist goes to brunch every weekend with her mother.[17] In 2006's *Something Blue*, Emily Griffin's protagonist, Darcy, also brunches.[18] The back cover of Norma Jarrett's 2004 novel, *Sunday Brunch: A Novel* reads: "*Waiting to Exhale* meets *Church Folk* as five female attorneys do brunch each week to trade tales about their love lives, law firms, and the Lord!"[19] Judith Marks-White's 2008 novel

Bachelor Degree features numerous brunch scenes, including one at New York City's Popover Café.[20] In *Nils, Ginger and Charlie* by Caro Somers, Nils and Ginger announce their wedding engagement over Christmas brunch.[21]

Several other books with brunch titles and themes overlap with women's literature and popular fiction. *Brunch of the Dead* by Bonner and Morgenstern is a novel about zombies that is really a critique of how to treat senior citizens.[22] *Sunday Brunch* by Ethelin Ekwa is a collection of poetry that features brunch.[23] *A Mobster's Menu for Mother's Day Brunch* by Beth Mathison in 2011 is a crime novel about a dysfunctional family.[24] *Memoir of the Sunday Brunch* by Julia Pandl is a memoir of serving brunch in a family restaurant.[25]

Children's books also have brunch themes. *Fancy Nancy's Marvelous Mother's Day Brunch* is a children's book about a child surprising her mother with a brunch.[26] *Brontosaurus Brunch* by Judi Peers and Mary Coles is a children's book about a dinosaur brunch.[27]

BRUNCH IN BOOKS AND NEWSPAPERS

Brunch began to appear in newspapers by the 1930s and continued to be featured in food and fashion magazines. Brunch was often part of Mother's Day or Easter features, which included recipes as well as tips about brunch etiquette. *New York Magazine* featured brunch as early as 1970. By the 1990s, brunch had taken on a gendered aspect in American culture. Many of the women who lunched until the 1950s became working women who brunched on the weekends.

In response, food magazines have increased their coverage of brunch in the last three decades and have published several cookbooks. In 1980, Sunset published *Sunset Brunch Cookbook: Make-Ahead Ideas, Menu Planning, Breakfast Surprises*. Break-

fasts and Brunches was published by *Bon Appétit. Brunch Menus (Great Meals in Minutes)* and *Weekends Are Entertaining: From Cocktail Parties and Brunches to Dinner for Two or Twenty (Everyday Cookbook)* were two of the earlier brunch books that were put out by Time-Life. More recently we have seen another influx of brunch cookbooks including *Food & Wine: 20 Best Breakfast and Brunch Recipes*, and *Joy of Cooking: All about Breakfast and Brunch. Breakfasts and Brunches* was another brunch cookbook published in 2005. Food and lifestyle magazines' compilations of recipes on brunch also include *Gourmet Every Day Meals, Hors d'Oeuvres, Salads, Main Courses, Side Dishes, Breakfast/Brunch, Desserts*, and *Marie Claire Style: Brunches*.

As more people eat brunch out and, in some cases, plan their weekends around their brunch plans, brunch guides have increased in popularity. Travel books, specifically books on New York City, often have entire sections dedicated to brunch, but more recently books on brunch have also become more prevalent. Several books dedicated to just brunching in New York including *New York's 50 Best Places to Enjoy Breakfast and Brunch: The Guide to the Best Morning Meals in the Big Apple, New York's 50 Best Places to Eat Brunch*, and *Brunch Secrets New York City: EAT (Deck of Secrets)*.

INTO THE TWENTY-FIRST CENTURY: BRUNCH IN SOCIAL MEDIA, BRUNCH BLOGS, AND FOOD WEBSITES

More recently brunch blogs, food websites, and Twitter feeds have played a significant role in preparing brunch at home or reviewing brunch restaurants. Brunch blogs offer recipes, and food and cooking websites provide a diverse variety of brunch possibilities. Twitter feeds on Sunday often include suggestions for brunch at home. The *New York Times* food and wine Twitter feed suggests brunch at home can be as simple as bagels and cream cheese. Melissa Clark writes:

> There are some who think a platter of bagels, cream cheese and lox is an ideal self-contained meal. Add some whitefish salad, sliced onion, tomatoes and maybe a small bowl of capers and you're done, without even turning on the stove. This said, there are times when I have family and friends coming over that I like to do it up. By filling out the offerings and keeping them fresh and inventive, I can serve what is my absolute favorite meal over and over again, for breakfast, lunch or dinner, without anyone getting tired of it. When I'm serving bagels and lox for dinner, in particular, I always include plenty of vegetables and salads to lighten things up. . . . And by the way, when New Yorkers say bagels and lox, we don't always strictly mean the salty pickled belly meat of the salmon, which is what traditional Jewish lox is. The word lox also colloquially means any kind of cold smoked salmon that you'd eat on a bagel (hot smoked salmon is a whole other thing). In general, true lox is saltier than most kinds of smoked salmon. I always order at least two varieties of smoked salmon and let my guests compare and contrast. . . . And that's another great thing about serving bagels and lox for a crowd—the leftovers might be even better enjoyed all by yourself.[28]

Brunch blogs continue to grow in influence. Blogs and Twitter feeds reflect brunch food trends, provide recipes, and even suggest brunch menus. *Epicurious* regularly shares ideas for brunch at home.[29] *Food 52* also has an active Twitter feed.[30] Following food sites or food writers on Twitter often provides suggestions for brunch at home or where to eat the next on-trend brunch. Brunch recipe sites and blogs can also give us pointers on how to create some of the best brunches at home. *Iheartbrunch.com* includes brunch recipes for making at home such as challah French toast.[31] *Brunch and the City* is another brunch blog that is written by a Washington, D.C., brunch blogger and has a great section of brunch recipes that include Valentine's Day waffles, French toast, and turkey hash. [32] We can often get the inspiration for brunch at home by looking through brunch blogs or food websites. In addition to brunch blogs, online news and food sites are also sources for recipes for cooking brunch at home. Brunch at home can be casual or formal, all American or ethnic. Brunch can be a time to experiment with diverse recipes at home

Other brunch blogs review brunches out in restaurants. The *BrunchGang NYC* is run by several friends who brunch in New York City. Their site includes the ten commandments for brunching, which includes their brunch reviews and experiences. [33] They rank their brunch meals out based on a mimosa rating system in which five mimosas is "the best of the best" and one mimosa is "you wish you were somewhere else for brunch." *Bitches Who Brunch* is a brunch and fashion blog that focuses on brunching out in Washington, D.C., and fashion. [34]

Brunch also pops up on Twitter quite often and recently the coolest brunch created a buzz across the Internet when Carrie Brownstein, Kim Gordon, Amy Poehler, and Aimee Mann shared pictures of themselves brunching. Carrie Brownstein (from *Portlandia* fame) tweeted: "One-Non Blonde plus three hotties. Brunch!" Buzzfeed referred to this brunch as "the coolest brunch in the history of brunch." [35]

Brunch also made the fake news, when the satirical *Onion* covered brunch recently, claiming that "affluent" children need their brunch. A brunch of French brioche and smoked salmon accompanied by live jazz music is what every "affluent" American child deserves:

> Declaring that every affluent child in America has the right to
> a well-balanced brunch, the U.S. Department of Agriculture
> announced the launch of a $40 million school brunch program
> aimed at distributing brioche French toast and smoked salmon
> to the nation's richest school districts. "We found that 70 per-

cent of students in wealthy communities were not receiving their recommended allowance of eggs Benedict and fresh-squeezed orange juice," Agriculture Secretary Tom Vilsack told reporters Friday. "Quite simply, we believe all children of privilege deserve a proper, well-composed brunch plate with complimentary jalapeno cornbread mini muffins and honey butter on the side. With this new program, we can finally begin to offer the superior culinary experience that until now has been sorely missing in school cafeterias from Greenwich, CT to Palo Alto, CA." Department officials said that if its brunch program proves successful, they remain open to the possibility of spending an additional $80 million annually to add live jazz music.[36]

Perhaps a parody in the *Onion*, means that brunch has really arrived?

THE FUTURE OF BRUNCH

Is brunch a civilized way to enjoy a meal with family and friends? Emily Post certainly changed her mind on the meal. Or is brunch as ridiculous and pretentious as shows like *Portlandia* portray? Some, like chef Anthony Bourdain, hate brunch; others will wait more than ninety minutes for the perfect, on-trend brunch.

The spread of brunch has been shaped by social class, gender, and religious norms. Brunch began on Sundays and then became a ritual shared on both Saturdays and Sundays. Globalization and colonialism both contributed to brunch's spread across the world, especially into parts of Asia and the Middle East, where brunch is often eaten on Sunday but also on Fridays in Muslim and Middle Eastern cultures.

Globalization and changes in the economy are also linked to meal patterns. We see the increase of global chains in both food and fashion. When Laduree, and later Maison Eric Kayser (the artisan French bakery), came to New York many of us rejoiced, while others were saddened by the McDonaldization (or global-ization) of the French pastry industry. McDonald's in Paris was initially met with protest, but now fast food is commonplace there. But even in France there is also a fairly new food move-ment. Michelin might be around for a very long time, but Adam Gopnick emphasizes that the Le Fooding movement focusing on artisan casual dining has moved in.[37]

The brunch meal will continue to reflect food trends, and also continue to be indicative of conspicuous consumption. There is nothing subtle about brunch. I am not sure if there is a more over-the-top brunch than what exists in Dubai. Dubai has per-haps out-brunched the West through its lavish champagne brunches and culinary indulgences. Will Mumbai be the next place that excels at the excess of Dubai? As a leisure class emerges, brunch follows. In the end, brunch is the meal of those with disposable time or disposable income, often with an affec-tion for indulgent or comfort food. When else during the week can you have steak and eggs with donuts and croissants, and even a drink before noon? There's no need to choose between savory and sweet during brunch; this is the midday meal when you can have both. But you are what you eat, if not at least metaphorically.

Food consumption has been linked to identity for years. Brunch consumption has been linked to class, gender, religion, and social norms. Those that are particularly aspirational, such as the creative and the middle class, will continue to brunch. Per-haps, brunch will become gender neutral, so that "dudes can brunch," but brunch may remain a way to mark religious and cultural holidays such as Christmas, Eid, and Hanukah. Those of us who increasingly feel the time crunch will continue to go out for holiday brunches. But at the same time, some middle-class Americans are slowing down and responding to Michael Pollan's thesis that we should be cooking at home for ourselves using local and organic ingredients.[38] Others will be cooking and eating together by hosting brunch potlucks in their neighborhoods. However, Julier points out that even potlucks are embedded with status markers.[39] Who brings and makes the gluten-free quiche, the organic turkey sausage, the artisan popovers, and the heirloom tomato salad is all coded with social meaning (ethnicity, class, and often gender). Class in particular continues to shape if we brunch, where we brunch, and what we consume at brunch. Brunch is a place where we overtly display our culinary capital.

Culinary capital is how we are able to raise our cultural capital or class distinction through our knowledge or consumption of food.[40] Will meals remain a way to achieve status or distinction?[41] Where we eat brunch reveals social and cultural capital. Why else would we make reservations five weeks in advance to brunch at the Flying Fig in Cleveland, Three Acres in Chicago, or Locanda Verde in Manhattan? Consumption is linked to identity, and not only what we eat, but where we eat says something about who we are, or who we think we are, or who we want to be.

Brunch continues to absorb ethnic, authentic, and exotic food trends as well. In London, you can enjoy a Pakistani-inspired brunch at Tayab's, or when in Mumbai you can have an Asian-inspired sushi brunch at the Four Seasons Mumbai. In many ways, brunch is the ultimate meal, in which you can really indulge in all your culinary cravings for exotic or local comfort foods. Today hipster brunches have spread from New York to London to Paris. Thomas Chatterton recently wrote in the *New York Times*: "People say you had to be in Paris in the '20s or New York in the '80s. The sad truth of our contemporary moment seems to be only that you no longer need to be anywhere in particular anymore. The brunch is all the same."[42] I surely hope this isn't so. Brunch is social, brunch can be decadent, and when else can you have organic waffles and local fried chicken and end with an artisan New York City cronut?[43]

Food cycles, like fashion cycles, follow trends—Southern food, ethnic food, hybrid food—it's all cyclical. We often search into the past for the next big trend—heirloom produce, heritage livestock, or historic recipes.[44] Brunch will continue to evolve and globalize. But the future often longs for something from the past, something that actually may never have existed.[45]

The future of brunch will be a hybrid of what we wish we were: diverse, global, authentic, and ethical. Brunch in the next decades will fuse locavore, artisan, and organic food trends to the ethnic cuisine of the next on-trend immigrant cuisine. As South Asian and Middle Eastern cultures increase in popularity in Western culture, we'll see more high-end Indian bistros, but the halal food trucks will be adding falafel brunch burritos to their menus. Ultimately, we'll all be waiting in ninety-minute lines at the Water Street Café in the Oneota Community Food Co-operative for an authentic and exotic brunch comprised of hand-crafted brunch rotis filled with eggs from local and cage-free chickens and keema[46] sourced from heritage SeedSaver cows accompanied by organic sweet parathas. Others of us will be driving through a Chick-fil-A for a chicken and biscuit sandwich.

RECIPES

Chai spiced French toast
Serves 4
Ingredients

- 4 large eggs
- 1 cup full-fat milk (or heavy cream)
- ½ tsp cinnamon
- ¼ tsp ground cardamom
- Pinch of nutmeg
- Pinch of ground ginger
- ¼ tsp ground clove
- 8 thick slices challah or brioche bread
- 4 tbsp unsalted butter, plus additional for buttering toast
- Seasonal fruit for serving
- Marmalade or maple syrup for serving

Directions

1. Preheat oven to 300 degrees.
2. In a bowl, whisk together the eggs, milk, cinnamon, nutmeg, ginger, clove, and cardamom. Dip both sides of bread slices in mixture until evenly distributed.

3. Melt the butter in a large nonstick skillet over medium heat, and cook the bread 2 slices at a time, until slightly browned (about 1 to 1½ minutes a side).
4. Butter each side of the toast and arrange on a large baking sheet, not touching each other, and bake 15 minutes until browned.
5. Garnish with fresh seasonal fruit and serve with marmalade (or maple syrup).

Garlicky scrambled eggs with fresh cilantro
Serves 4

Ingredients

- 8 large eggs
- ¼ tsp salt
- ¼ tsp red chili powder
- ¼ tsp turmeric
- 2 tbsp butter
- 2 garlic cloves, finely chopped
- ½ medium onion, finely chopped
- ⅓ cup finely chopped fresh cilantro

Directions

1. In a bowl, beat together the eggs, and spices until blended.
2. Melt the butter in a nonstick pan over medium heat, then reduce the heat to low. Add the garlic and onion; and cook, stirring until lightly browned, about 2 minutes, then add the beaten eggs to the onions and garlic and cook until eggs are set, for about 3 minutes.
3. Add the cilantro, and cook about 2 minutes more.
4. Divide the scrambled eggs among 4 plates, and serve with naan or zeera aloo (cumin potatoes).

Pumpkin spice pancakes
Serves 4
Ingredients

- 1¼ cups all-purpose flour
- 1 tbsp brown sugar
- 2 tsp baking powder
- ½ tsp cinnamon
- ¼ tsp ground ginger
- ¼ tsp nutmeg
- ¼ tsp cardamom
- ¼ tsp salt
- Pinch of ground clove
- 1 cup buttermilk
- 6 tbsp canned pumpkin puree
- 2 tbsp softened salted butter
- 1 large egg
- 2 tbsp of butter for frying
- Butter and maple syrup for serving

Directions

1. Whisk together flour, brown sugar, baking powder, and the spices in a large bowl.
2. In a separate bowl, whisk together buttermilk, pumpkin, softened butter, and egg.
3. Add wet ingredients to dry and stir with a whisk until it comes together to form a batter.
4. Heat a nonstick skillet over medium heat, then add butter to skillet and allow to melt, turning the skillet to coat the bottom completely.
5. Pour in ⅓ cup of batter for each pancake.

6. Cook pancake until brown and then flip to cook the other side.

Baked chole (curried chick peas and sweet potatoes)
Serves 6
Ingredients

- 2 large sweet potatoes, diced
- 1 cup canned chick peas, rinsed and drained
- 1 small onion, chopped
- 2 cloves garlic, finely chopped
- 3 tbsp olive oil
- 2 tsp cumin
- 1 tsp turmeric
- ½ tsp ground coriander
- 2 tsp salt
- Garnish: chopped fresh Cilantro

Directions

1. Preheat oven to 350 degrees.
2. Toss all ingredients except cilantro and spread on a large baking sheet. Bake until potatoes are golden, about 30 minutes.
3. Garnish with fresh cilantro and serve with naan and masala omelet.

Cumin potatoes (zeera aloo)
Serves 4
Ingredients

- 3 tbsp of olive oil
- 1 lb small potatoes, sliced medium

- 2 cloves garlic, sliced thinly
- 1 large yellow onion, sliced thinly
- ½ tsp salt
- 1 tsp cumin
- 1 tsp turmeric
- 3 dried red peppers

Directions

1. Heat oil in skillet over medium heat.
2. Add garlic and onions and cook until slightly brown.
3. Add spices and toss with garlic and onions.
4. Add sliced potatoes to skillet and fry until golden brown.
5. Serve with eggs and naan.

Yasmeen's masala omelet
Serves 2
Ingredients

- 5 large eggs
- 2 tbsp of olive oil
- 2 garlic cloves, sliced
- 1 small onion, finely chopped
- 1 hot green chili pepper, finely chopped
- ½ tsp salt
- ¼ tsp mirchi (red chili pepper)
- ½ tablespoon fresh cilantro, finely chopped

Directions

1. Pour oil in a nonstick pan over medium heat, then add garlic and onion. Cook, stirring occasionally until lightly browned.

2. Meanwhile, in a medium bowl, beat eggs with green chili pepper, salt, and mirchi. Add chopped cilantro.
3. Pour eggs into the pan with garlic and onions.
4. Cook until set on the sides.
5. Using a spatula, flip omelet and cook until completely set.
6. Serve with naan and cumin potatoes or baked chole.

NOTES

I. BRUNCH HISTORY

1. William Grimes, "At Brunch, the More Bizarre the Better," *New York Times*, July 8, 1998.

2. Colin Spencer, *British Food: An Extraordinary Thousand Years of History* (London: Grub Street Publishing, 2002), 260–61.

3. "News and Notes for Women, 1896," *New Oxford*, November 27, 1896.

4. Rien Fertel, "Brunch," in *Entertaining: From Ancient Rome to the Super Bowl*, ed. Melitta Weiss Adamson and Francine Segan, 2 vols. (Westport, CT: Greenwood Press, 2008), 1:93–94.

5. John Egerton, *Southern Food: At Home, on the Road, in History* (Chapel Hill: University of North Carolina Press, 1993), 58.

6. Louise McKinney, *New Orleans: A Cultural History* (Oxford: Oxford University Press, 2006), 36–37.

7. Egerton, *Southern Food*, 58.

8. Madame Begue was a German immigrant to New Orleans who catered to French merchants and her "second breakfast" was influenced by both French and German traditions.

9. Herman B. Deutsch, *Brennan's New Orleans Cookbooks* (New Orleans: Robert L. Crager & Company, 1964), 25.

10. Deutsch, *Brennan's New Orleans Cookbooks*.

11. Deutsch, *Brennan's New Orleans Cookbooks*, 26.

12. Judy Walker, Ann Maloney, and Karen Taylor Gist, "Best of the Brunch for Sundays: When Breakfast, Lunch and Jazz Converge," *Times Picayune*, www.nola.com/dining/index.ssf/2010/11/post_6.html.

13. Egerton, *Southern Food*; Seb Emina and Malcolm Eggs, *The Breakfast Bible* (London: Bloomsbury, 2013).

14. Peter Joseph Khali and Salma Khali, *Boozy Brunch: The Quintessential Guide to Daytime Drinking* (Lanham, MD: Taylor Trade Publishing, 2012), 18.

15. Lately Thomas, *Delmonico's: A Century of Splendor* (Boston: Houghton Mifflin Harcourt, 1967).

16. Thomas, *Delmonico's*.

17. Fertel, "Brunch," 94.

18. Thomas Doremus and Russell Maloney, "'Benedict,' Talk of the Town," *New Yorker*, December 19, 1942.

19. Gregory Beyer, "Was He the Eggman?," *New York Times*, April 8, 2007, Section 14, 1; Doris Tobias, "Perfect Eggs Benedict," *Bon Appétit*, March 1978, 53–54, 98.

20. Andrew Smith, *The Oxford Companion to American Food and Drink* (Oxford: Oxford University Press, 2007), 87.

21. David J. Hanson, "Temperance Movement Groups and Leaders in the U.S.," *Alcohol Problems and Solutions*, www2.potsdam.edu/hansondj/Controversies/1124913901.html#.Us05VfRDvNk.

22. For more on temperance and prohibition see Eric Burns, *The Spirits of America: A Social History of Alcohol* (Philadelphia: Temple University Press, 2004); David J. Hanson, *Preventing Alcohol Abuse: Alcohol, Culture, and Control* (Westport, CT: Praeger, 1995), chap. 3; Herbert Asbury, *The Great Illusion: An Informal History of Prohibition* (1950; repr. New York: Greenwood Press, 1968); and John Kobler, *Ardent Spirits: The Rise and Fall of Prohibition* (New York: G. P. Putnam's Sons, 1973).

23. Catherine Gilbert Murdock, *Domesticating Drink: Women, Men, and Alcohol in America, 1870–1940* (Baltimore: Johns Hopkins University Press, 1998), 109; Lori Rotskoff, *Love on the Rocks: Men, Women, and Alcohol in Post–World War II America* (Chapel Hill: University of North Carolina Press, 2001).

24. Andrew Smith, *Drinking History: Fifteen Turning Points in the Making of American Beverages* (New York: Columbia University Press, 2013), 145; Melissa Shedden, "*Great Gatsby* Fever Makes Bloody Mary

the Hottest Drink Choice of 2013, Say Britain's Top Bartenders," *Mail Online*, March 28, 2013, www.dailymail.co.uk/femail/article-2300673/Great-Gatsby-fever-makes-Bloody-Mary-hottest-drink-choice-2013-say-Britains-bartenders.html.

25. Shedden, *"Great Gatsby* Fever."

26. Linda Stradley, "Bacon Bloody Mary Cocktail—Bacon Infused Vodka," *What's Cooking America*, http://whatscookingamerica.net/Beverage/Bacon-BloodyMary.htm.

27. Joseph Carlin, *Cocktails: A Global History* (London: Reaktion Books), 2012.

28. Culinary Institute of America, *Culinary Institute of America: Breakfast and Brunches* (New York: Lebhar-Friedman Books, 2005), 28.

29. Marjorie Hillis and Bertina Foltz, *Corned Beef and Caviar (For the Live Aloner)* (Indianapolis, IN: Bobbs-Merrill, 1937), 111–12.

30. Hilary Schenker, "1970s," in *American Food by the Decades*, ed. Sherri Liberman (Santa Barbara, CA: Greenwood, 2001), 175.

31. Ida C. Bailey Allen, *Mrs. Allen on Cooking, Menus, Service* (New York: Doubleday, 1924), 872.

32. George Frederick Scotson-Clark, *Half Hours in the Kitchenette: A Self Help for Small Families* (New York: D. Appleton, 1925), 13.

33. Della Thompson Lutes, "A Breakfast Party," What the Gracious Host Says, *Fayete (Iowa) County Leader*, January 20, 1927.

34. Ann Batchelder, "We Call It Brunch," *Delineator*, May 1932, 29.

35. Della Thompson Lutes, *The Gracious Hostess: A Book of Etiquette* (Indianapolis, IN: Bobbs-Merrill, 1923), 79.

36. Ruth Chambers, "Modern Hostess Turns to Social Breakfasting," *Washington Post*, October 24, 1933.

37. Dorothea Duncan, "Combining Breakfast, Luncheon Ideal for Adults on Christmas Day," *Washington Post*, December 23, 1935.

38. Dorothy Marsh, "How We Abolished Week-End Drudgery at Our Home," *Portsmouth Times*, July 19, 1936.

39. Martin Ellyn, "Brunch Replacing Early Breakfasts," *Washington Post*, September 11, 1937.

40. Emily Post, "Breakfast or Lunch," *Syracuse Herald*, October 9, 1936.

41. Martin Ellyn, "Guests May Come Before or After Church, Luncheon May Be Double Duty Event, Eggs Are Featured on All Menus," *Washington Post*, April 7, 1939.

42. "For Gourmets and Others Sunday Morning Brunch," *New York Times*, February 12, 1939, 55.

43. Home Institute, *Young America's Cookbook* (New York: Scribners, 1938), 63.

44. Louise Price Bell, *Successful Parties* (New York: Fleming H. Revell, 1940), 63.

45. Jessie DeBoth, "Leisurely Breakfast on Sunday," *Boston Globe*, April 13, 1941, B52.

46. Ruth Berolzheimer, ed., *The Breakfast and Brunch Cook Book* (Chicago: Consolidated Book Publishers, 1942), 31.

47. Berolzheimer, *The Breakfast and Brunch Cook Book*, 31.

48. Katherine Fisher, "Sunday-Morning Brunch Equals Breakfast and Lunch," *Good Housekeeping*, June 1945, 81–82.

49. Fannie Engles, *Fannie Engles' Cookbook* (New York: Essential Books, Duell, Sloan, and Pearce, 1946), xl.

50. Theresa Nefy, "We Switched to Sunday Brunch," *Parents' Magazine & Family Home Guide*, June 1957, 32, 66–84.

51. Time-Life, *Picture Cook Book* (New York: Time-Life, 1958), 103.

52. Dorothy Marsh, *Good Housekeeping Cookbook* (New York: Harcourt Brace and World, 1955), 608.

53. Carol Brock, "For the Hostess: Brunches," *Good Housekeeping*, May 1955, 154.

54. Ira Krasnow, "America's Brave New Meal," *Chicago Tribune*, June 30, 1980.

55. "Be a Carefree Weekend Hostess at Brunch," *American Home*, June 1964, 57.

56. Robert Sepper, "Fort Lauderdale: Brunch, an American Tradition," *Ladies Home Journal*, 1966, 83.

57. Nancy Gray, "Come to Brunch," *American Home*, November 1967, 58.

58. Helen Gurley Brown, *Single Girl's Cookbook* (New York: Bernard Geis Associates, 1969), 363.

59. Brown, *Single Girl's Cookbook*, 363.

60. June Roth, foreword to *June Roth's Let's Have a Brunch Cookbook* (New York: Essandess Special Edition, 1971).

61. Jeanne McClow, *McCall's Beautiful Brunch Book* (New York: Saturday Review Press, 1972), 3.

62. Anita Borghese, *The Great Sandwich Book* (New York: Rawson Associates, 1978), 100–101.

63. Krasnow, "America's Brave New Meal," 11.

2. CULTURAL IMPORTANCE IN THE UNITED STATES AND AROUND THE WORLD

1. *Brunch Menus* (New York: Time-Life Books, 1984), 7.

2. Linda Civitello, *Cuisine and Culture: A History of Food and People* (New York: John Wiley & Son, 2011), 307.

3. Diana Butler Bass, "The Radical History of Mother's Day," *Huffington Post*, May 11, 2013, www.huffingtonpost.com/diana-butler-bass/radical-history-of-mothers-day_b_3259326.html.

4. "Menus and Recipes," *Philadelphia Tribune*, May 8, 1948, 8.

5. Civitello, *Cuisine and Culture*, 308.

6. Lynn Stewart, "Brunch on New Year's Day," *American Home*, January 1948, 83.

7. Craig Claiborne, "Easter Brunch," *New York Times Magazine*, March 30, 1958, 63.

8. Jacqueline De Goumois Bloch, "Brunch and Supper Parties in Your Own Back Yard," *Parents Magazine and Family Home Guide* 34 (July 1959): 64.

9. Lillian Langseth-Christensen and Carol Sturm Smith, *The Brunch Cookbook* (New York: Walker, 1968), 9.

10. Peggy Post, *Emily Post's Wedding Etiquette*, 4th ed. (New York: William Morrow, 2006).

11. Nancy Tuckerman and Nancy Dunnan, *The Amy Vanderbilt Complete Book of Etiquette: 50th Anniversary Edition* (New York: Doubleday, 1995), 200.

12. Egg bakes are a Midwestern egg casserole. They can be found in small towns and throughout rural Iowa, Minnesota, and Illinois, www.midwestliving.com/travel/missouri/st-louis/hotels/dwell-912/ (for recipe seehttp://thomsonhouse.biz/recipes/).

13. Joel Denker, *The World on a Plate: A Tour through the History of America's Ethnic Cuisine* (New York: Basic Books, 2003).

14. Adrian Pasquarelli, "Donuts, the New Cupcake," *Crain's New York Business*, July 22, 2012, www.crainsnewyork.com/article/20120722/SMALLBIZ/307229974.

15. Paula Forbes, "No, Donuts Are Not the New Cupcake," *Eater*, July 23, 2012, http://eater.com/archives/2012/07/23/no-doughnuts-are-not-the-new-cupcake.php.

16. Jessica Sidman, "Holier Than Thou: How Two New Fried Chicken and Doughnut Spots Compare," *Washington City Paper*, December 6, 2012, www.washingtoncitypaper.com/blogs/youngandhungry/2012/12/06/holier-than-thou-how-two-new-fried-chicken-and-doughnut-spots-compare/.

17. "Cronut Craze Takes Over Manhattan," CBS News New York, http://newyork.cbslocal.com/2013/06/07/cronut-craze-takes-over-manhattan/.

18. Allan Davidson, *The Penguin Companion to Food*, rev. ed. (New York: Penguin Books, 2002).

19. Jessie Rhodes, "Scrapple: The Meatloaf of the Morning," *Smithsonian*, November 8, 2011, http://blogs.smithsonianmag.com/food/2011/11/scrapple-the-meatloaf-of-the-morning/.

20. Aubrey Nagle, "Six Pack: Scrapple Whether You Like It or Not," *Foobooz*, August 3, 2008, www.phillymag.com/foobooz/2012/08/03/six-pack-scrapple-whether-you-like-it-or-not/.

21. Andrew Smith, *The Oxford Companion to American Food and Drink* (Oxford: Oxford University Press, 2007), 69, 113.

22. Torey Avey, "Discover the History of Chicken and Waffles," *The History Kitchen*, January 18, 2013, www.pbs.org/food/the-history-kitchen/history-chicken-and-waffles/2/.

23. John Folse, *Hot Beignets and Warm Boudoirs: A Collection of Recipes from Louisiana's Bed and Breakfasts* (Gonzales, LA: Chef John Folse and Co., 1999), 6, 9.

24. *West Union United Methodist Church Millennium Cookbook* (Kearney, NE: Morris Press, 2000.

25. Bloch, "Brunch and Supper Parties in Your Own Back Yard," 64.

26. "Best Toronto Brunch 2013: 20 Top Brunch Picks from HuffPost Foodies," *Huffington Post*, June 21, 2013, www.huffingtonpost.ca/2013/06/21/best-toronto-brunch-2013_n_3467985.html.

27. Jeffrey Pilcher, *Que Vivan Los Tamales: Food and the Making of Mexican Identity* (Albuquerque: University of New Mexico Press, 2008).

28. Pilcher, *Que Vivan Los Tamales*, 136.

29. Laura Mason, *Food Culture in Great Britain* (Westport, CT: Greenwood, 2004), 137.

30. Mason, *Food Culture in Great Britain*.

31. Seb Emina, *The Breakfast Bible* (New York: Bloomsbury, 2013).

32. Ed Mahon, *Land of Milk and Honey: The Story of Traditional Irish Food and Drink* (Dublin: Poolbeg Press).

33. Farm Restaurants, www.thefarmfood.ie/?p=255.

34. The Merrion, www.merrionhotel.com/sunday_brunch_2.php.

35. See Michaela DeSoucey, "Gastronationalism: Food Traditions and Authenticity Politics in the European Union," *American Sociological Review* 75, no. 3 (June 2010): 432–55.

36. Bob Morris, "Hangovers and Leftovers," *New York Times*, May 8, 2005, www.nytimes.com/2005/05/08/fashion/sundaystyles/08age.html?_r=0.

37. Civitello, *Cuisine and Culture*, 388.

38. "Hollandaise. One of the most prominent sauces in the group of those which are thickened by the use of egg yolk. The fact that such a sauce will curdle if heated beyond a certain point is largely responsible for their reputation of being difficult. McGee . . . has investigated both the history and the chemistry of the sauce. He reports that one of the earliest versions which he found, 'sauce a la hollandoise,' in the 1758 edition of Marin's *Dons de Comus*, calls only for butter, flour, bouillon, and herbs; no yolks at all. . . . Sauces which are derived from, or can be regarded as variations of, hollandaise include: sauce aux capres, maltaise, mousseline, moutarde (Dijon mustard)." Alan Davidson, *Oxford Companion to Food* (Oxford: Oxford University Press, 1999), 383. Food Timeline states: "Food historians generally agree that Hollandaise sauce was a French invention, most likely dating to the mid-18th century. Why the reference to Holland? This country (or more broadly the Netherlands) was famous for its fine butter and good eggs." Food Timeline, http://www.foodtimeline.org/foodsauces.html#hollandaise.

39. Lindsey Tramuta, "Brunch on a Budget in Paris's 10th Arrondissement," *T: New York Times Style Magazine*, June 28, 2012, http://

tmagazine.blogs.nytimes.com/2012/06/28/brunch-on-a-budget-in-pariss-10th-arrondissement/.

40. Cornelia Jarosch, "Viennese Cuisine with History: The Viennese 'Gabelfrühstück,'" *Vienna Insight*, April 18, 2012, www.vienna-insight.at/2012/04/18/viennese-cuisine-with-history-the-viennese-gabelfruhstuck/.

41. "Dubai's Outlandish Brunch Culture," *Huffington Post*, February 9, 2013, http://www.huffingtonpost.com/departures-magazine/friday-brunch-in-dubai_b_2638125.html.

42. Krishnendu Ray and Tulasi Srinivas, *Curried Cultures: Globalization, Food, and South Asia*, California Studies in Food and Culture (Berkeley: University of California Press, 2012).

43. Chitrita Banarji, *Eating India* (New York: Bloomsbury, 2007), 83.

44. Banarji, *Eating India*, 94.

45. Madhur Jaffrey, *From Curries to Kebabs* (New York: Clarkson Potter, 2003), 114.

46. Jaffrey, *From Curries to Kebabs*, 115.

47. Jaffrey, *From Curries to Kebabs*, 118.

48. Madhur Jaffrey, *Indian Cooking* (New York: Barrons, 1994), 66.

49. Pushpa Bhargava, *From Mom with Love: Complete Guide to Indian Cooking and Entertaining* (Nesconset, NY: Crest Books, 2009).

50. Meenakshi Agarwal, *Indian Cooking: A Step-by-Step Guide to Authentic Dishes Made Easy* (Guilford, CT: Knack, 2010), 146.

51. "The Wild Brunch: The Fight to Fill the Stomachs of Mumbai's Rich," *Economist*, July 6, 2013, www.economist.com/news/asia/21580513-fight-fill-stomachs-mumbais-rich-wild-brunch.

52. Naushaba Tabassum, "Pakistani Breakfast," IFood.tv, www.ifood.tv/blog/pakistani-breakfast.

53. Su Hyun Lee, "A New Lifestyle in South Korea: First Weekends and Now Brunch," *New York Times*, November 2, 2007, www.nytimes.com/2007/11/02/world/americas/02brunch.html.

54. Leslie Gourse, "Dim Sum Has Come a Long Way, from Esoteric to Mass Popularity," *Chicago Tribune*, March 13, 1988, http://articles.chicagotribune.com/1988-03-13/travel/8802290511_1_dim-sum-yum-cha-chinese-cooking.

55. Zoe Li, "How to Eat Dim Sum: The Best Five Dishes," *CNN Travel*, September 6, 2012, http://travel.cnn.com/how-to-eat-dim-sum-377769.

56. "Menu: Dim Sum Brunch at Home," *Saveur*, May 10, 2012,www.saveur.com/article/Menu/Dim-Sum-Brunch.

57. Lisa Heldke, *Exotic Appetites: Ruminations of a Food Adventurer* (New York: Routledge, 2003).

3. BRUNCH AT HOME

1. "Summer Brunch Recipes: How to Throw a Party at Breakfast-Time," *Huffington Post*, August 15, 2013, www.huffingtonpost.com/2013/08/15/summer-brunch-recipes-breakfast-party_n_3757005.html?ncid=edlinkusaolp00000003.

2. Mary Foote Henderson, *Practical Cooking and Dinner Giving: A Treatise Containing Practical Instructions in Cooking . . .* (New York: Harper and Brothers, 1889).

3. James Beard, *The Complete Cookbook for Entertaining* (Indianapolis, IN: Bobbs-Merrill Company, 1954), 19

4. Beard, *The Complete Cookbook for Entertaining*, 19.

5. Craig Claiborne, "After the Easter Parade," *New York Times Magazine*, April 3, 1966, 86.

6. "Progressive Easter Brunch," *Sunset*, April 1954, 192.

7. "Wedding Breakfast," *San Antonio Light*, June 14, 1938.

8. Emily Post, "Good Taste Today," *Manitowoc (Wisconsin) Herald Times*, December 14, 1942.

9. Betty Crocker Editors, *Betty Crocker's Hostess Cookbook* (New York: Golden, 1967), 73.

10. Betty Crocker Editors, *Betty Crocker's Hostess Cookbook*, 72.

11. Betty Crocker Editors, *Betty Crocker's Hostess Cookbook*, 79.

12. Laura Shapiro, *Something from the Oven: Reinventing Dinner in 1950s America* (New York: Penguin, 2005).

13. "Poppy Cannon's Viennese Brunch," *Milwaukee Sentinel*, September 4, 1970.

14. Susannah Blake, *Easy Breakfast and Brunch: Simple Recipes for Morning Treats* (London: Ryland Peters and Small, 2007), 7.

15. Emily Matchar, *Homeward Bound: Why Women Are Embracing the New Domesticity* (New York: Simon & Schuster, 2013).

16. Melanie De Proft, ed., *Brunch, Breakfast and Morning Coffee* (Chicago: Culinary Arts Institute, 1955), 3.

17. Pat Jester, *Brunch Cookery* (Tucson, AZ: HP Books, 1979), 6.

18. Jester, *Brunch Cookery*, 2.

19. "How to Set a Pretty Table for a Sunday Brunch Buffet," *Real Simple*, www.realsimple.com/home-organizing/how-to-set-a-pretty-table-10000001729339/page3.html.

20. Rachel White, "How to Host a Spring Brunch," *Huffington Post*, April 9, 2012, www.huffingtonpost.com/Menuism/hosting-a-spring-brunch_b_1409192.html.

21. yummytummy, "Table Setting for Brunch," Ifood.tv, May 30, 2011,www.ifood.tv/blog/table-setting-for-brunch#F3XOsAPKrGGjAbJQ.99.

22. Susan Spungen, *What's a Hostess to Do?* (New York: Artisan Books, 2013), 207.

23. Randy James, "The White House Easter Egg Roll," *Time*, April 13, 2009, http://content.time.com/time/nation/article/0,8599,1890844,00.html#ixzz2glP1yd6M.

24. "The White House Easter Egg Roll," White House Historical Association, www.whitehousehistory.org/whha_press/index.php/backgrounders/white-house-easter-egg-roll/.

25. Lynn Sweet, "Sweet: Menu for the White House 2008 Easter Brunch," *Chicago Sun Times*, March 22, 2008, http://blogs.suntimes.com/sweet/2008/03/sweet_menu_for_the_white_house.html.

26. Tammy Haddad, "The Garden Brunch History: How a Back Yard Get-Together Turned into a Tradition," *WHCD Insider*, www.whitehousecorrespondentsweekendinsider.com/dinner-history/the-garden-brunch/.

27. "Celebrating the 20th Annual White House Garden Brunch," *WHCD Insider*, April 25, 2013, www.whitehousecorrespondentsweekendinsider.com/2013/04/25/celebrating-the-20th-annual-white-house-garden-brunch/.

28. Ruth Berolzheimer, ed., *The Breakfast and Brunch Cook Book* (Chicago: Consolidated Book Publishers, 1942), 31.

29. Claiborne, "After the Easter Parade," 86.

30. Berolzheimer, *The Breakfast and Brunch Cook Book*, 31.

31. De Proft, *Brunch, Breakfast and Morning Coffee*, 3.

32. Christopher Cavanaugh, *Brunches and Lunches: America's Best-Loved Community Cookbook Recipes* (New York: Meredith, 1996), 7.

33. Michael McLaughlin, *Good Mornings: Great Breakfasts and Brunches for Starting the Day Right* (San Francisco: Chronicle, 1996), 82.

4. BRUNCH AWAY FROM HOME

1. "The Sunday Brunch," *Time*, October 21, 1966, 98.

2. Gael Greene, *Bite: A New York Restaurant Strategy for Hedonists, Masochists, Selective Penny Pinchers and the Upwardly Mobile* (Toronto: J. McLeod Ltd., 1971), 297.

3. William Grimes, "At Brunch, the More Bizarre the Better," *New York Times*, July 8, 1998, www.nytimes.com/1998/07/08/dining/at-brunch-the-more-bizarre-the-better.html?pagewanted=all&src=pm.

4. Grimes, "At Brunch, the More Bizarre the Better."

5. Roger Sands, "Executive Chef David Garcelon Oversees Venerable Sunday Brunch in NYC Waldorf Astoria," *Just Luxe*, August 28, 2013, www.justluxe.com/lifestyle/dining/feature-1949492.php.

6. Joshua Estrin, "Sunday Brunch at the Waldorf Astoria Is Not to Be Missed," *Huffington Post*, January 2, 2013, www.huffingtonpost.com/joshua-estrin/waldorf-astoria-brunch_b_2381103.html.

7. Florence Fabricant, "Uptown, Downtown," *New York Magazine*, May 28, 1979, 51–57.

8. "The Sunday Brunch," *Time*.

9. John R. Walker, *The Restaurant: From Concept to Operation* (New York: John Wiley and Sons, 2007).

10. Charles Ranhofer, *The Epicurean: A Complete Treatise of Analytical and Practical Studies on the Culinary Art . . .* (New York: Charles Ranhofer, 1894).

11. Greene, *Bite*, 301.

12. Gaynor Maddox, "Leisurely Saturday Brunch Is In," *Leader Herald* (Gloversville, NY), March 4, 1965.

13. Maddox, "Leisurely Saturday Brunch Is In."

14. Greene, *Bite*, 299.

15. Frank Rosario, "The Kitchen Is Closed at Fables Rainbow Room," *New York Post*, January 12, 2009, http://nypost.com/2009/01/12/the-kitchen-is-closed-at-fabled-rainbow-room/.

16. Greene, *Bite*, 299–300.

17. "Lou Mitchell's Restaurant, Chicago, Illinois," in *Route 66: Discover Our Shared Heritage Travel Itinerary*, National Park Service, www.nps.gov/nr/travel/route66/lou_mitchells_chicago.html.

18. "Walker Bros. Marks 50th Anniversary with—What Else?," *Wilmette Life*, May 13, 2010, 5.

19. For more on the history of pancakes, see Ken Albala, *Pancake: A Global History* (London: Reaktion Books, 2008).

20. Christopher Borrelli, "'Funkalicious' Eclectic Global Cuisine: Evanston's Lucky Platter Resembles a Cool Flea Market and the Food Is Tasty Too," *Chicago Tribune*, March 29, 2012, http://articles.chicagotribune.com/2012-03-29/features/ct-dining-0329-home-plate-lucky-20120329_1_tin-ceiling-ed-paschke.

21. Big Jones brunch menu, www.bigjoneschicago.com/brunch.html.

22. Jeff Houck, "Brunch Is Back: Tampa Bay Chefs Get Creative," *Tampa Tribune*, March 28, 2013, http://tbo.com/dining/brunch-is-back-tampa-bay-chefs-get-creative-b82469141z1.

23. Houck, "Brunch Is Back."

24. See www.calvarynaperville.org/resources/food.

25. See www.asburydenton.org/asbury-fellowship-brunch-february-26th-1000-a-m.

26. Geoffrey A. Fowler, "Brunch as a Religious Experience Is Disturbing Berkeley's Karma," *Wall Street Journal*, February 10, 2009, http://online.wsj.com/news/articles/SB123422026431565295.

27. Claire Moses, "Brunch and History at the Hoboken Synagogue," *Hoboken Patch*, January 14, 2010, http://hoboken.patch.com/groups/opinion/p/brunch-and-history-at-the-hoboken-synagogue.

28. Fabricant, "Uptown, Downtown," 52.

29. Linda Vongkhamchanh, "Best Kept Brunch Secret: Untitled at The Whitney," *1st Look Best Kept Secrets*, NBC Bay Area, August 10, 2012, www.nbcbayarea.com/blogs/1st-look/Best-Kept-Brunch-Secret-Untitled-at-The-Whitney-155786295.html.

30. Elena Paravantes, "A Traditional Greek Breakfast Now Offered at the Acropolis Museum in Athens," *Olive Tomato*, February 6, 2013,

www.olivetomato.com/eat-a-real-greek-breakfast-at-the-acropolis-museum-in-athens/#ixzz2nGwwD200.

31. See www.wwltv.com/news/French-Quarter-Fest-Music-lineup-map-food-vendors--198790631.html.

32. "Mr. Kelly Debuts Jazz Brunch," *Chicago Defender*, March 20, 1971, 16.

33. "Mr. Kelly Debuts Jazz Brunch," *Chicago Defender*.

34. Frances Frank Marcus, "New Orleans Up Close: Jazz and Eggs Over Easy," *New York Times*, August 14, 1988.

35. Mark Huntsman, "Crawfish Boils, Jazz Brunches, and Reveillon Dinners: The Role of Tradition and Change in Three Ritual Meals from Louisiana," *What's Cooking in America*, http://whatscookingamerica. net/MarkHuntsman/CrawfishBoil_JazzBrunch_ReveillonDinner.htm.

36. Huntsman, "Crawfish Boils, Jazz Brunches, and Reveillon Dinners."

37. Leslie Gourse, "Gospel on the Menu," *Los Angeles Times*, April 5, 1998, http://articles.latimes.com/1998/apr/05/travel/tr-36136.

38. "Sylvia's Queen of Soul Food Restaurant," *Food Communities of NYC*, http://macaulay.cuny.edu/eportfolios/lobel11neighborhoods/ harlem/food-stops-in-harlem/sylvias-queen-of-soul-food-restaurant/.

39. John Spacey, "The Strange Story of Japanese Vikings," *Japan Talk*, February 21, 2012, www.japan-talk.com/jt/new/strange-story-of-Japanese-vikings.

40. Beth Reiber, *Frommer's Tokyo*, Frommer's Complete Guides (Hoboken, NJ: Wiley, 2008).

41. Debasmita Ghosh, "Egg-ing on Easter," *Hindustan Times*, March 28, 2013, www.hindustantimes.com/Entertainment/Art/Egg-ing-on-Easter/Article1-1033668.aspx.

42. Georgina Wilson-Powell, "Brunch Gets Civilized in Dubai," *The Passport Blog*, BBC, December 13, 2012, www.bbc.com/travel/blog/ 20121211-brunch-gets-civilized-in-dubai.

43. Wilson-Powell, "Brunch Gets Civilized in Dubai."

44. Joanna Kakissis, "36 Hours in Athens, Greece," *New York Times*, May 4, 2008, www.nytimes.com/2008/05/04/travel/04hours.html? pagewanted=all&_r=0.

45. "What's on the Menu for Easter Sunday in Puerto Rico?," *Examiner*, March 30, 2012, www.examiner.com/article/what-s-on-the-menu-for-easter-sunday-puerto-rico.

46. Jeffrey M. Pilcher, *Food and the Making of Mexican Identity* (Albuquerque: University of New Mexico, 1998), 136.

5. BRUNCH IN POPULAR CULTURE

1. *The Simpsons*, "Life on the Fast Lane," season 1, episode 9 (1990).

2. *Seinfeld*, "The Invitations," season 7, episode 22 (1996).

3. *The Big Bang Theory*, "The Bakersfield Expedition," season 6, episode 13 (2013).

4. *Arrested Development*, "Out on a Limb," season 2, episode 11 (2002).

5. *LA Story*, Steve Martin, wr., Mick Jackson, dir. (1991; USA: Lion's Gate Home Entertainment, 2006), DVD.

6. See Peter Naccarato and Kathleen LeBesco, *Culinary Capital* (New York: Berg, 2012), which builds on Bourdieu's concept of cultural capital.

7. *Frazier*, "The Whine Club," season 7, episode 17 (2000).

8. *Will and Grace*, "The Needle and the Omelet's Done," season 5, episode 7 (2002).

9. *Gossip Girls*, "The Wild Brunch," season 1, episode 2, (2007).

10. *Sex and the City*, "Attack of the Five Foot Ten Woman," season 3, episode 3 (2000).

11. *30 Rock*, "Stride of Pride," season 7 , episode 3 (2012).

12. *How I Met Your Mother*, "World's Greatest Couple," season 2, episode 5 (2006).

13. *The Mary Tyler Moore Show*, "Ted's Wedding," season 6, episode 9 (1975).

14. *The Hangover Part II*, Todd Philips, dir. (2011; Warner Home Video), DVD.

15. Melissa Banks, *The Girls' Guide to Hunting and Fishing* (New York: Penguin, 2000), 97–98.

16. Pamela Hollins, *No; Maybe Yes* (Lincoln, NE: iUniverse, 2001).

17. Jennifer Weiner, *Good in Bed* (New York: Washington Square Press, 2002).

18. Emily Griffin, *Something Blue* (New York: St. Martin's, 2006).

19. Norma Jarrett, *Sunday Brunch: A Novel* (New York: Broadway Books, 2004).

20. Judith Marks-White, *Bachelor Degree* (New York: Ballantine, 2008).

21. Caro Somers, *Nils, Ginger and Charlie* (n.p.: BookSurge Publishing, 2008).

22. Sean Bonner and Allen Morgenstern, *Brunch of the Dead* (n.p.: Surprise Attack Press, 2013).

23. Ethelin Ekwa, *Sunday Brunch* (n.p.: PublishAmerica, 2009).

24. Beth Mathison, *A Mobster's Menu for Mother's Day Brunch* (n.p.: Fingerprints, 2011).

25. Julia Pandl, *Memoir of the Sunday Brunch* (Chapel Hill, NC: Algonquin Books, 2012).

26. Jane O'Connor, *Fancy Nancy's Marvelous Mother's Day Brunch* (New York: HarperFestival, 2011).

27. Judi Peers and Mary Coles, *Brontosaurus Brunch* (n.p.: byDesign Media, 2011).

28. Melissa Clark, "Setting Out the Bagels and Lox," *New York Times*, September 24, 2013.

29. "Tomato Egg Cups (photo)," Eggs for Breakfast and Brunch slideshow, *Epicurious*, www.epicurious.com/recipesmenus/slideshows/eggs-for-breakfast-and-brunch-52261?slide=1&slideRecipeTitle=Tomato-Egg-Cups.

30. See http://food52.com/.

31. See http://iheartbrunch.com/category/easy-brunch-ideas/.

32. See http://brunchandthecity.com/category/recipes/

33. See http://brunchgang.com/10-commandments-of-brunch/.

34. See http://bitcheswhobrunch.com/about-us/.

35. Matthew Perpetua, "The Coolest Brunch in the History of Brunch," BuzzFeed, September 15, 2013, www.buzzfeed.com/perpetua/the-coolest-brunch-in-the-history-of-brunch.

36. "USDA Rolls Out New School Brunch Program for Wealthier School Districts," *Onion*, April 26, 2013, www.theonion.com/articles/usda-rolls-out-new-school-brunch-program-for-wealt,32218/?ref=auto.

37. Adam Gopnik, "No Rules! Is Le Fooding, the French Culinary Movement, More Than a Feeling?," *New Yorker*, April 5, 2010, www.newyorker.com/reporting/2010/04/05/100405fa_fact_gopnik.

38. Michael Pollan, *Cooked: A Natural History of Transformation* (New York: Penguin, 2013).

39. Alice Julier, *Eating Together: Food, Friendship and Inequality* (Urbana: University of Illinois Press, 2013).

40. Naccarato and LeBesco, *Culinary Capital*.

41. Josee Johnston and Shyon Baumann, *Foodies: Democracy and Distinction in the Gourmet Foodscape* (New York: Routledge, 2009).

42. Thomas Chatterton, "How Hipsters Ruined Paris," *New York Times*, November 8, 2013, www.nytimes.com/2013/11/10/opinion/ sunday/how-hipsters-ruined-paris.html?_r=0.

43. The cronut is a trademarked creation of Dominique Ansel.

44. According to Seed Savers Exchange outside Decorah, Iowa, "An heirloom variety is a plant variety that has a history of being passed down within a family or community, similar to the generational sharing of heirloom jewelry or furniture. An heirloom variety must be open-pollinated, but not all open-pollinated plants are heirlooms" (Christy, "The Difference between Open-Pollinated, Heirloom, and Hybrid Seeds," Seed Savers Exchange, MAy 2, 2012, http://blog.seedsavers.org/ open-pollinated-heirloom-and-hybrid-seeds/).

45. Stephanie Coontz, *The Way We Never Were: American Families and the Nostalgia Trap* (New York: Basic Books), 1993.

46. Ground meat cooked in Indian spices usually garam masala/garlic and onions.

SELECTED BIBLIOGRAPHY

Albala, Ken. *Pancake: A Global History*. London: Reaktion Books, 2008.

Banarji, Chitrita. *Eating India: An Odyssey into the Food and Culture of the Land of Spices*. London: Bloomsbury, 2007.

Beard, Jim. *The Complete Cookbook for Entertaining*. Indianapolis, IN: Bobbs-Merrill, 1954.

Berolzheimer, Ruth, ed. *The Breakfast and Brunch Cook Book*. Chicago: Consolidated Book Publishers, 1942.

Better Homes and Gardens. *Lunches and Brunches*. New York: Meredith Press, 1963.

Brown, Helen Gurley. *Single Girl's Cookbook*. New York: Bernard Geis Associates, 1969.

Burns, Eric. *The Spirits of America: A Social History of Alcohol*. Philadelphia: Temple University Press, 2004.

Civitello, Linda. *Cuisine and Culture: A History of Food and People*. New York: Wiley, 2011.

Collingham, Lizzie. *Curry: A Tale of Cooks and Conquerors*. Oxford: Oxford University Press, 2007.

Davidson, Allan. *The Penguin Companion to Food*. Rev. ed. New York: Penguin Books, 2002.

DeSoucey, Michaela. "Gastronationalism: Food Traditions and Authenticity Politics in the European Union." *American Sociological Review* 75, no. 3 (2010): 432–55.

Denker, Joel. *The World on a Plate: A Tour through the History of America's Ethnic Cuisine*. New York: Basic Books, 2003.

Deutsch, Hermann B. *Brennan's New Orleans Cookbooks*. New Orleans: Robert L. Crager & Company, 1964.

Egerton, John. *Southern Food: At Home, on the Road, in History*. Chapel Hill: University of North Carolina Press, 1993.

Emina, Seb, and Malcolm Eggs. *The Breakfast Bible*. London: Bloomsbury, 2013.

Engles, Fannie. *Fannie Engles' Cook Book*. New York: Essential Books, Duell, Sloan, and Pearce, 1946.

Fertel, Rien. "Brunch." In *Entertaining: From Ancient Rome to the Super Bowl*. 2 vols. Edited by Melitta Weiss Adamson and Francine Segan. Westport, CT: Greenwood Press, 2008.

———. "Begué's Eggs." In *Eggs in Cookery: Proceedings on the Oxford Symposium on Food and Cookery, 2006*. Edited by Richard Hosking. London: Prospect Books, 2007.

Folse, John. *The Encyclopedia of Cajun and Creole Cuisine*. New Orleans: Chef John Folse & Co., 2004.

Greene, Gael. *Bite: A New York Restaurant Strategy for Hedonists, Masochists, Selective Penny Pinchers and the Upwardly Mobile*. Toronto: J. Mcleod Ltd., 1971.

Grimes, William. *Appetite City: A Culinary History of New York*. New York: North Point Press, 2010.

Harris, Jessica. *High on the Hog: A Culinary Journey from Africa to America*. New York: Bloomsbury, 2011.

Heldke, Lisa. *Exotic Appetites: Ruminations of a Food Adventurer*. New York: Routledge, 2003.

Herrick, Christine. *What to Eat, How to Serve It*. New York: Harper & Brothers, 1891.

Jester, Pat. *Brunch Cookery*. Tucson, AZ: HP Books, 1979.

Julier, Alice. *Eating Together: Food, Friendship and Inequality*. Urbana: University of Illinois Press, 2013.

Khali, Peter Joseph, and Salma Khali. *Boozy Brunch: The Quintessential Guide to Daytime Drinking*. Lanham, MD: Taylor Trade Publishing, 2012.

Langseth-Christensen, Lillian, and Carol Sturm Smith. *The Brunch Cookbook*. New York: Walker, 1968.

Lutes, Della Thompson. *The Gracious Hostess: A Book of Etiquette*. Indianapolis, IN: Bobbs-Merrill, 1923.

Mahon, Ed. *Land of Milk and Honey: The Story of Traditional Irish Food and Drink*. Dublin: Poolbeg Press, 1991.

Naccarato, Peter, and Kathleen LeBesco. *Culinary Capital*. New York: Berg, 2012.

Pilcher, Jeffrey M. *Food and the Making of Mexican Identity*. Albuquerque: University of New Mexico Press, 1998.

Ray, Krishnendu, and Tulasi Srinivas. *Curried Cultures: Globalization, Food, and South Asia*. California Studies in Food and Culture. Berkeley: University of California Press, 2012.

Roth, June. *June Roth's Let's Have a Brunch Cookbook*. New York: Essandess Special Edition, 1971.

Rotskoff, Lori. *Love on the Rocks: Men, Women, and Alcohol in Post–World War II America*. Chapel Hill: University of North Carolina Press, 2001.

Shapiro, Laura. *Something from the Oven: Reinventing Dinner in 1950s America*. New York: Penguin Books, 2005.

Smith, Andrew. *The Oxford Companion to American Food and Drink*. Oxford: Oxford University Press, 2007.

Spencer, Colin. *British Food: An Extraordinary Thousand Years of History*. London: Grub Street Publishing, 2002.

Thomas, Lately. *Delmonicos: A Century of Splendor*. Boston: Houghton Mifflin Harcourt, 1967.

Tuckerman, Nancy, and Nancy Dunnan. *The Amy Vanderbilt Complete Book of Etiquette: 50th Anniversary Edition*. New York: Doubleday, 1995.

Walker, John R. *The Restaurant: From Concept to Operation*. New York: Wiley, 2007.

INDEX

ABOUT THE AUTHOR

Farha Ternikar is an associate professor of sociology at Le Moyne College where she teaches Food and Culture, Gender and Society, and the Sociology of Food. She has authored several articles on ethnicity and immigrant identity in the *Journal of Ethnic Studies*, *International Journal of Contemporary Sociology*, and *Sociology Compass*, and most recently her research was included in the 2012–2013 exhibit *Lunch Hour NY: The New York Public Library*.